Alfred the Great

 LFRED

THE

GREAT

by Eleanor Shipley Duckett

THE UNIVERSITY OF CHICAGO PRESS

CHICAGO AND LONDON

ISBN: 0-226-16777-1 (clothbound); 0-226-16779-8 (paperbound)

THE UNIVERSITY OF CHICAGO PRESS, CHICAGO 60637
The University of Chicago Press, Ltd., London

TO NORA KERSHAW CHADWICK

with admiration and gratitude

"He that hewed timber afore out of the thick trees: was known
to bring it to an excellent work." *Psalm 74, verse 6: Book of Common Prayer*

Foreword

THIS IS A VERY simple book. It is offered to those—
and, of course, they are many in these busy days—who, if
they were suddenly asked just what the name of Alfred
the Great meant to them, would promptly answer with
one or more of the following: "He conquered the Danes,
whoever they were in those times." "Wasn't he the king
who burned some cakes in some woman's cottage?" "He
dressed up as a minstrel and spied upon the enemy's
camp." "He cut out White Horses in the hills to cele-
brate his victories." "The tower in the park, the tearoom
in the village, the statues in some towns, and the daffodils
in my garden are named after him." "Didn't he translate
some old books?" "Was he the king who started England's navy?" "Did he invent trial by jury?" All these
answers are honored by tradition; they rest, some on
truth, some on romanticism; and all are dealt with here in
their proper places.

In the late nineteenth century the historian John Richard Green wrote of this king of Wessex: "The love
which he won a thousand years ago has lingered round
his name from that day to this. While every other name
of those earlier times has all but faded from the recollec-
tion of Englishmen, that of Ælfred remains familiar to

every English child." I doubt whether Green's statement is true of today.

Anglo-Saxon England, the England before, during, and after Alfred's time, has been splendidly described within recent years. One has only to mention, among those known for the revealing of its history, the names of Sir Frank Stenton, of R. H. Hodgkin, of Sir Arthur Bryant, of Dorothy Whitelock, of Peter Hunter Blair, of D. J. V. Fisher, and of John Pope.

There are also many "Lives" of Alfred in our libraries. But the best of these biographies were written many years ago, before the writers mentioned above had given us their views based upon their research. Perhaps, then, this book, which gladly acknowledges its debt to them, will not be out of place among those who grew up, or did not grow up, with the legends of Alfred the Great at school. It has three aims: to do what it may in spreading among us the knowledge of this king who did so much for his England and his world; to place him in his setting—Saxon, Celtic, and Continental; and to build his story on simple lines, which rest nevertheless upon a foundation suggested by the sources given at its close.

As with my former books on Anglo-Saxon life and personalities, many friends and scholars on both sides of the Atlantic have here once more given me that help and encouragement for which I am deeply grateful. For invaluable criticism of this book in typescript I wish to thank especially Bruce Dickins, Elrington and Bosworth Professor of Anglo-Saxon in the University of Cambridge.

E. S. D.

Contents

Maps

ENGLAND
DURING THE SUPREMACY
OF OFFA OF MERCIA
IN 796 A.D.

ALFRED'S WARS
AGAINST THE DANES
869–78 A.D.

Firth of Forth

STRATHCLYDE

Tyne

NORTHUMBRIA

IRISH SEA

York
YORKSHIRE

Humber

Torksey
LINDSEY
Lincoln

The Wash

MERCIA

Nottingham
Derby
Repton
NOTTS

DERBYSHIRE

EAST
ANGLIA

CAMBRIDGE · Thetford
Cambridge

WALES

*Mouth of
the Stour*

DYFED

Severn Gloucester
GLOUCESTER
Circencester ASHDOWN
Chippenham

London

Wedmore
BERKSHIRE Reading
Rochester

Bristol Channel

WILTS
Edington
SOMERSET · Athelney HAMPSHIRE

Canterbury
KENT

Thames

DEVON
·Exeter Wareham·

CORNWALL

ENGLISH CHANNEL

FRANCE

DIVISION OF ENGLISH LAND
BY THE PEACE OF 886 A.D.
BETWEEN KING ALFRED
AND THE DANES

NORTHUMBRIA

DANES

YORKSHIRE

IRISH SEA

Humber

Mersey

DANISH

Trent

LINCOLN

The Wash

ANGLESEY

GWYNEDD

MERCIA

POWYS

ENGLISH

EAST

DEHEUBARTH

MERCIA

WATLING ST.

ANGLIA

DANES

WALES

DYFED

ESSEX

MORGANNWG

Severn

GLOUCESTER

Thames

London

BERKSHIRE

SURREY

KENT

WILTS

WESSEX

SOMERSET

HAMPSHIRE

SUSSEX

DEVON

DORSET

CORNWALL

ENGLISH CHANNEL

FRANCE

LATER WARS
OF KING ALFRED
AGAINST THE DANES
892–96 A.D.

NORTHUMBRIA

DANES

DANISH
MERCIA

Chester

ENGLISH
MERCIA

EAST
ANGLIA

DANES

Buttington

SHROP SHIRE

Severn

Bridgnorth

WATLING ST.

Bedford

WALES

Essex

Mersea Isle

Shoebury

Leu

London Benfleet

Sheppey

Thames

Isle of
Thanet

Berkshire Farnham

Rochester

Milton

Wilts

Surrey

Lymphe

Somerset

Hampshire

Appledore

Devon

Dorset

Exeter

ENGLISH CHANNEL

FRANCE

Alfred the Great

KINGS OF WESSEX

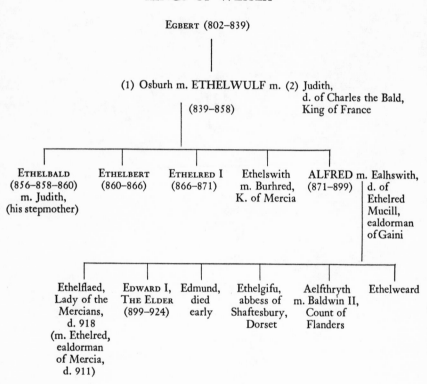

EGBERT (802–839)

(1) Osburh m. ETHELWULF m. (2) Judith,
(839–858)   d. of Charles the Bald,
            King of France

ETHELBALD   ETHELBERT   ETHELRED I   Ethelswith   ALFRED m. Ealhswith,
(856–858–860)   (860–866)   (866–871)   m. Burhred,   (871–899) d. of
m. Judith,   K. of Mercia   Ethelred
(his stepmother)   Mucill,
                                                                       ealdorman
                                                                       of Gaini

Ethelflaed,   EDWARD I,   Edmund,   Ethelgifu,   Aelfthryth   Ethelweard
Lady of the   THE ELDER   died   abbess of   m. Baldwin II,
Mercians,   (899–924)   early   Shaftesbury,   Count of
d. 918   Dorset   Flanders
(m. Ethelred,
ealdorman
of Mercia,
d. 911)

CHAPTER ONE

Wessex BEFORE THE TIME OF ALFRED

THE NINTH CENTURY in all its course was the century of Alfred the Great. Its first half, from 800 to 849 A.D., saw, as it were, the preparation of the theater, the gradual building of the background, in England, Scotland, Ireland, and Wales, in France, in Germany, in Scandinavia. Against this background, of invasion and of war, of destruction and of lawlessness, of constant struggle on English soil between the foreign intruder and the native-born, of ignorance deep and universal, ignorance concerning the things of God and of man, this king played his leading part, and for the high manner of his playing stands alone among the rulers of English land.

We begin our story, then, in the first years of this ninth century: in 802, to be exact, the year in which Egbert, Alfred's grandfather, came on the scene as ruler of Wessex, the kingdom of the West Saxons. As its king he governed in the south and west of England the shires of Somerset, Dorset, and Devon, Wiltshire and Hampshire. In Cornwall the Celtic British were still holding out against West Saxon conquest, and Berkshire was a debatable region, swaying between West Saxon and Mercian control.

In these years, indeed, the word "Mercian" meant much to Wessex, for the kings of Wessex, one after another, acknowledged the supremacy of Mercia, the Midland kingdom of the Trent Valley. This power of overlordship had been won during the previous, the eighth, century by those great rulers of Mercia, Ethelbald and his more famous successor, Offa. Offa, as king of Mercia, at his death in 796 had been not only lord of Mercia proper, in the lands of Stafford, Derby, Nottingham, Warwick, Worcester, and Leicester. His power as supreme head was also acknowledged among all peoples south of the river Humber; from what is now Lincolnshire to the Middle and the East Anglians, to the border peoples of Cheshire, Shropshire, and Hereford, to the men who dwelt about the Severn, to the Angles of Kent, to the Saxons of the east, the middle, the south, and the west. London itself was a Mercian city.

Such was still the position of Wessex when Egbert, Alfred's grandfather, came to its throne. The history of his coming holds interest for us. Sixteen years before this time, in 786, he had laid claim to this throne as one of direct descent in the royal House of Wessex as well as a prince of Kent. His claim was strong. But it had met a stronger force. In this same year of 786 the crown of Wessex was gained by one named Beorhtric, a man of obscure ancestry but fortunate in the support of Offa himself, king of Mercia and overlord of Wessex. Offa had sealed this alliance in 789 by giving to Beorhtric his daughter, Eadburh, in marriage. Promptly Egbert fled from England to find refuge among the Franks at the court of Charles the Great, and Beorhtric remained king of Wessex for these sixteen years.

In 802 Beorhtric suddenly died. The manner of his dying, strange and violent, if we may believe the gossip down the years of West Country tradition, brings King Alfred into our story. Long afterward Alfred told all that he himself had heard about it to his friend and counselor, Asser of Wales, and we still have Asser's reporting of the tale. Alfred told, and Asser must have hung upon his words, that the Lady Eadburh, after her marriage to Beorhtric, had become so haughty and overbearing toward her husband at the Wessex court that she did everything in her power to injure anyone for whom he cared. She also accused of evil in his presence all who had in any way offended her, hoping to deprive them of influence or even of life. If her efforts failed, men declared, she slipped poison into their drink; and one day her husband, King Beorhtric, drank by mistake of the cup which she had poisoned for another and so came to his end.

Her own end, Alfred went on to tell, was even more miserable. After Beorhtric's death she packed up all her jewels and other valuable possessions and crossed with them to the court of King Charles in Frankland. And, as she stood before him, holding out many gifts in hope of his friendship, the king said: "Choose which of us you will, Eadburh, either me or this son of mine who stands here by my side."

In her folly, said Alfred, she answered, with never a

moment's hesitation: "If choice be given me, I choose your son, for he is younger than you."

Then Charles answered her with a smile and said: "If you had chosen me, you should have had my son. Now, for this choosing which you have made, you shall have neither of us." He thereupon sent her to a convent of nuns, who in their reverence for her high birth made her their abbess; but her evil heart led her into sin with a man of her own country. She was cast out, and she ended her days as a beggar on the street corners of Pavia in Italy.

The rule of Wessex now lay open to Egbert. At his accession, like Beorhtric, he knew Mercia as overlord. But Egbert was no son-in-law of a Mercian king, bound by gratitude; on the contrary, that very Mercian king had driven him from his country and from the throne he claimed. The years of his exile, moreover, had done much for him. He was now immeasurably stronger and wiser, far more ambitious to extend his kingdom's holding. Not in vain had he watched Charles the Great, king and emperor, ruling Franks and Saxons of France and of Germany and many other nations which had been subdued in many campaigns, administering law, exacting allegiance from people and from nobles alike.

Now, then, during the thirty-six years of the rule of Wessex by this ancestor of Alfred, we are to trace the turn of the tide in his kingdom, from subjection to Mercia to a new independence, a freedom from Mercian power. No doubt Egbert rejoiced as in a happy omen when, on the very day of his enthroning, his men of Wiltshire routed and drove back the Mercian invaders who were hurrying to raid Wessex fields.

Yet he waited long for decisive action, perhaps that he might gather his strength and abide his hour. At last, when in 815 the Celts of Cornwall rose against the West Saxons who were steadily encroaching upon their land and liberty, he marched to work destruction in Cornwall from east to west and made over to the West Saxon church a tenth part of that land.

Ten years later, in 825, Egbert was ready for war against his overlord, the king of Mercia, at this time one Beornwulf by name. Their armies met at "Ellendun," now known as Wroughton near Swindon in Wiltshire. The battle was decisive. Beornwulf was conquered, and threefold fruit of victory fell into Egbert's hands. The men of East Anglia yielded to him their homage and service; secular rule over Kent, Essex, Sussex, and Surrey now passed to Wessex as a lasting heritage of its kings; and henceforth Wessex was free from the supremacy of the Mercian throne. Four more years went by, and in 829 Egbert attained his highest hope. Again he met Mercia's army and Mercia's king, now one Wiglaf, in another great battle, and now he conquered Mercia itself.

This victory over Wiglaf, it is true, did not bear permanent result. In the course of time the Mercian kings regained their crown and much of its substance, held sway as of old over Middlesex and London and Berkshire, and commanded homage in matters of the church from the bishops of Kent and Sussex, including Canterbury.

Egbert, however, successfully continued to extend his power. In this same year of 829 his presence at the head of his army at Dore in Derbyshire brought the men who lived in Northumbria, north of the river Humber, to peace and submission to his will. The following years he won the same from the Welsh by marching into Wales. Lastly, before he died he led his army a second time into Cornwall against the Celtic Cornishmen, still stubbornly resisting the West Saxon invaders, and completed their subjection to his rule by a new victory at Hingston Down.

Egbert, then, had followed the inspiration of his friend and protector, Charles the Great, so far as his power of mind and character could carry him. His kingdom had been delivered from Mercian control; the boundary of its rule and influence had been greatly extended; and its repute among Englishmen was now far higher than he had found it at his coming.

2

Egbert died in 839, and his son Ethelwulf followed him on the royal throne of Wessex. History remembers Ethelwulf as the father of Alfred the Great and, more generously, as another leader in battle, though of far less achievement than Egbert. He had taken part in Egbert's wresting of supremacy from Mercia. At his father's command he had marched with Ealhstan, the fighting bishop of Sherborne, and with Wulfheard, "ealdorman," governor under the king, of Hampshire, at the head of a great army into Kent in 825; the passing of Kent and Essex and Sussex and Surrey from the rule of Mercia into the kingdom of greater Wessex had been in part carried out by him and his men. He himself had become ruler of these regions under King Egbert, and now in turn he gave them over to his own eldest son, Athelstan, to govern in the same minor way.

Ethelwulf was not, however, by nature a man of arms. His heart lay in the peaceful practice of devotion to the Catholic church, that church which from its head and center in Rome had taught and tended the peoples of England since the sixth century, which from the seventh century had seen bishop and clergy, monks and missionaries, in Wessex. This father of Alfred was destined by fate to do his best to defend his church and his land from sudden and savage attack; and it is to his credit that he met with courage, throughout much defeat and some success, the menace which was to fall upon his kingdom.

At the beginning of his reign he sent his envoys across the Channel on a mission to Frankland. These envoys found in the kingdoms of the Franks, in France and in Germany, a state of affairs very different from that of the time of Charles the Great. Charles had now been dead twenty-five years, and his son, Louis the Pious, had long been trying to hold together the Empire of the West. Louis, like Ethelwulf, was devout and eager in the service of the church; for her he poured out all he had, of time, of energy, of money. But he could not control his rebellious sons, Lothar and Louis the German, and their half-brother, Charles the Bald. Long before he died these three sons were quarreling in their haste to grasp the various lands of his empire, left finally at his death in 840 helpless against its disruption and its fall.

It was in 839, shortly before the death of Louis, that Ethelwulf as king of Wessex sent to ask of him permission to pass through the land of the Franks on his way to

Rome. He was going, he said, on a pilgrimage of prayer, for his people had been terrified by a vision revealed to a priest among them. An angel had appeared to this man of God, warning that the sins of Christian men were crying aloud in their iniquity and that even the prayers of the Holy Souls offered day by day for men's repenting could no longer hold back the wrathful justice of heaven. Already blight was falling upon the fields and orchards of England. Unless its people turned speedily to penitence and kept with due respect the days set apart for worship of the Lord, forthwith there would come upon them heathen men, with an immense multitude of ships, to destroy both the land and its inhabitants with fire and the sword.

Whatever the vision, its prophecy, its foreboding, was realized only too soon. It was in Ethelwulf's reign that the Vikings of Scandinavia first began in force that work of destruction which was to haunt and harry his son Alfred's life from childhood to death. Not for sixteen years was Ethelwulf himself able to leave England for pilgrimage of prayer at Rome.

3

The origin of the word "Viking" has been disputed. Scholars have explained it as meaning "one who frequents a creek or fjord," from the Old Norse *vik*, a bay; otherwise, as "a warrior," from the Old Norse *vig*, battle; and still otherwise, in connection with the Old English *wic*, a camp, as "one who came from a settlement to work havoc." But in any case the word from early medieval days came to mean everywhere "a pirate from overseas."

As such the Viking was pictured, by the Christian chroniclers who told his deeds, in the blackest colors of brutality, sacrilege, and all evil. And this was literally a truthful picture of these Scandinavian adventurers who during this ninth century overran Europe—France, Germany, Spain, the Netherlands, Russia, and the British Isles—who destroyed their harvests, stormed their towns, looted their holy places for the treasures these guarded, killed their priests, monks, and layfolk, and raped their women.

But the Vikings were only part of the Scandinavian picture and, moreover, were the cause in other ways of actual benefit to Europe. And since they were of so great import, for evil or for good, to England, Scotland, and Ireland of Alfred's day, it is well to place them against their Scandinavian background.

The dwellers in Scandinavia—Norway, Sweden, and Denmark—come to light in the Stone Age, roughly prior to 1500 B.C., as people hunting with arrows and harpoons of bone and horn the wild boar, the deer, and the wolf in their forests, the whale and the seal and lesser prey in their fjords and streams; raising wheat and barley in rude fields; tending among their huts and byres cattle, sheep, and pigs. During the thousand years that followed, from 1500 to 500 B.C., we see them plying their oars in primitive boats across the Baltic to meet traders from southern Europe, who brought them in exchange for furs and amber the bronze from which they now fashioned their weapons, their plows, trappings for their horses, and utensils for their daily need at home. During another thousand years, from 500 B.C. to 500 A.D., first, during the history of Rome as Republic, they were laying the foundations of their future prosperity; then, during the Roman Iron Age, they were building ships to sail the seas; commerce was carried on with traders of the Roman Empire; intercourse with Roman culture was giving them new inspiration for defense, for invention of things of practical necessity and things of artistic form. Already settlers were coming across the North Sea to join them, to take possession of land which lay within reach and only needed clearing.

This progress was far more marked in the period of the Great Migrations which heralded and followed the fall of Rome in the West, when barbarian peoples wandered north, and Scandinavian fighters drifted into barbarian hordes on the Rhine and the Danube to attack and raid the Roman armies in their latter years. It was not surprising that the treasures brought home as reward of battle should excite these men of Scandinavia, now growing from primitive energy of physical life into a mature ambition, a conscious desire, for the possession, for the actual creating in their own land, of the beauty and the luxury which they had found abroad, for the going-forth of their ships in search of new prizes, fresh models for their own increasing skill.

Legends from the sixth and seventh centuries A.D. tell of the Yngling line of kings of Sweden, of the Scylding dynasty in Denmark. But not until the Viking Age was at its dawn, about 800, can we think of Sweden as united under one king; and, except for Horik the Dane in the mid-ninth century, no power was to draw the people of Denmark together under one rule until long after Alfred lay dead.

The tradition of Norway's unifying as one kingdom is of special interest. About that same year of 800, on Norway's west coast, in the land of Vestfold which bordered on Oslo Fjord, there was ruling one Gudröd, of the old Swedish Yngling royal house. He was known to men as the Hunter King, and his queen was Asa, daughter of King Harold Redbeard. Story, fostered in Norway and in Iceland, declared that this King Harold had refused to give his daughter to Gudröd and that Gudröd had fallen upon him by night and killed him; that then in revenge Queen Asa sent a page of her household one evening to murder her husband as he was coming down the gangway from his ship, merry with feasting. She was his second wife, and it was their son, Halfdan the Black, and still more their grandson, Harold Fairhair, who during Alfred's reign were, one after the other, drawing Norway's jarls to submission to one single crown.

When the Younger Iron Age, which saw the Viking conquests, was beginning its course, also about that year of 800, Scandinavia was still parceled out in farms, and its people were still living on the soil. But the farms were steadily growing larger, as more and more forest land was cleared for use. On each individual farm lived the family which owned it, from the head, who held chief control, to his sons and sons-in-law, who dwelt on the same wide estate, shared in its farming, and shared, too, in the rights of its property. The heads of neighboring estates and their families and households met on days of feast in their common sanctuary for the worship of their gods, on days of council for the discussion of laws and secular affairs. Presiding over both, as priests, as judges, as leaders of debate, were the chieftains, the jarls, whose families owned the largest estates, who as warriors and administrators fulfilled somewhat the same offices as ealdormen in England.

Here, then, the youth of Scandinavia heard their chief men telling in their council, called the *thing*, of the marvels to be seen and possessed in foreign lands, of the adventures of their countrymen who had sailed far abroad in ships, to trade and to capture, and, as time went on, to settle and make new homes for themselves and their kindred. Here they bowed in the common temple of their families and neighbors before the images of their ancient gods: Othin, who gave wisdom for the council and skill for the battle; Thor, who gave man strength for the fight and for the winning of his daily bread; Frey, who made the harvest to grow into fruitfulness; Freyja, who defended the home. Here they saw the leaders of their people hold up to these gods in priestly office the sacrificial victim, bird or beast or even man, which should win for their land aid and success in peace and in war; here they themselves were sprinkled with the sacrificial blood; here they saw their warriors dedicate their service by solemn oath upon the holy ring, the armlet laid upon the altar; here they revered the spirits of the dead who had fought well and truly for their cause, now and then hoping that the joyous feast of Othin in Valhöll might be theirs thereafter.

Faith in these young men of Scandinavia held no account of meekness, of suffering in patience, of Christian resignation and fortitude, of selfless love. The gods rewarded those who went forth valiantly to conquer and to gain. Bloodshed and death were the paths which led to wealth and content, alike in this world and the next; and the battle yielded joy to the ruthless and the strong. So, as they believed, their own wise Othin had counseled, in the lessons of a poetry which has come to us from the centuries of Christian life and thought in Scandinavia, but which runs far back in tradition of word and spirit to earlier, pagan days:

The foolish thinks to live forever if he shun the battle: the spear may spare him, but old age will not.

He rises early who would win another's wealth or life.

Seek not to know thy fate, so shalt thou live freest from sorrow; but go not on thy way without thy spear.

Bloodshed and death, the joys of battle and conquest, and the rewards promised by the gods to valiant men were symbolized among these Scandinavian warriors by the prophetic bird of Othin, the raven, which flew in woven design upon their battle standards. Around this bird, believed to be endowed with magical wisdom and knowledge, have gathered stories of myth and saga. Sometimes, it was said, a battle standard was woven plain and bare, without design. When victory was coming to those who carried it on the field, a raven marvelously appeared upon this empty surface, rising on its talons in ecstasy of triumph, opening wide its beak, flapping its wings. When defeat was imminent, its form slowly grew clear on the same waving flag, but quiet and still, crouched with drooping head.

United with this spirit of war and adventure, and, indeed, furthered by it, was that Scandinavian impulse toward art and culture which was also rising in new birth from the first years of this ninth century. In its first quarter the poet Bragi was creating the earliest Skaldic verses we possess, himself the hero and forerunner of a long line of Skalds who sang in complex strain—lyric, narrative, satiric—of the high deeds of those Scandinavian kings whose devoted followers and counselors they were. Building, woodwork, weaving, painting of these early days have left behind them many witnesses to their worth. Most happily of all, time has revealed to us those ships in which the people of Scandinavia's Viking Age laid their dead: those who being dead yet lived vigorously within the burial mound, the *howe;* who, as men believed, came back from it to the world of their former life for the joy or the misery of their kindred still on earth.

Famous among these ships is that one in which the Queen Asa, of whom we have already heard, was buried, under a mound laid open in 1904 at Oseberg in Vestfold. Asa, murderess if she was, was a great lover of beautiful things, and in those treasures found in her grave, treasures which she had probably been gathering for many years, we have the high-water mark of the culture of the early Viking Age. Here were tapestries worked in various colors to bring to life Norse legends; a carriage and sledges, adorned with intricate carving; posts bearing the heads of animals, bizarre and baroque, but marvelously alive, breathing a spirit of menacing strength. The prow of this ship, which dates from about 800 A.D. and is now in the Oslo Museum, is rounded into a snail's whorl and ends in a serpent's head; its stern and crosspieces are also covered with that same richly carved decoration. It is extravagant; yet here can be seen an awareness in Viking Norway of both the classical legacy of Rome and the art of Carolingian times.

This energy, this culture, together with a zest for making new homes, new ordered settlements, new cities of their own, the young Scandinavian explorers and fighters carried far and wide in Europe. They raided and plundered for the sake of the wealth they coveted, but they organized trade routes; they gave, to the lands they visited with their destruction and on which they finally settled with their families, of their own skill in seafaring, of their own genius for promoting trade and industry; they opened up lands hitherto remote and connected them with the civilized world.

The motives which first drove them forth on their adventures across the seas are not difficult to understand. These young sons of Scandinavian families saw no future for themselves at home but to settle on the patriarchal estate in a minor position and a relatively small portion, in the midst and under the control of their elder kinsfolk. Did they purpose going out to seek other land in their own countries, they were met by a multitude of fellow-seekers, including those brought by the barbarian tide of immigration. Their own western coast, to which most of them belonged, was ill suited for farming. Seafaring was in their blood; the Iron Age had given them ships; traders and missionaries had told of the riches and treasures of the lands around the Mediterranean and even across the Atlantic. They left home, then, to explore, to know adventure, to gain land and wealth.

And, when they did steer their boats toward some foreign shore, they found little enough to resist them. England at this time had nothing which could be called a fleet, and its people were dreaming of anything but attack from the sea. Charles the Great, it is true, had been aware of Scandinavian menace. He had held armed truce with that fierce old warrior, the Danish king, Godfred, and each had built rampart against the other's attack. Had not Godfred with a laugh declared he would soon march into Aachen, the royal seat of Charles, at the head of his army? And had not Charles himself one day in France seen Viking raiders sailing from its coast and turned away to hide his angry tears? "I have no fear," he had said to his courtiers, "that those fools can do me harm; I weep, because they have dared to reach this shore, and I still live. What will they do to those who come after me?"

Yet Charles did far more harm than good in regard to Viking assault when he destroyed the power of Frisia in the Netherlands, where then dwelt a seafaring people which stood between this peril and his Frankish land. Thenceforward the way across the North Sea lay open. Louis the Pious, his son, had done what he held within him to do. He had listened to the plea of the Danish king, Harold the Second, for aid against his enemy rivals at home, had seen him baptized with magnificent ceremony at Mainz in 826, had given him land for his holding, and had sent the saintly Anskar home with him for the converting of his people. But the Scandinavians clung firmly to the old ways, and Anskar, as missionary bishop, found his life full of adventure and trial. Finally, after Louis died in 840, the discord and warring between his sons left France and Germany an easy prey.

4

The Vikings began quietly, seeking first of all to land and explore. They crossed the North Sea, put into the Shetlands, the Orkneys, and the Hebrides, and proceeded to occupy them. Thence in the early 800's they sailed on to Scotland and Ireland and tasted the joy of monastic prize in ransacking Iona and Clonmacnois, Moville and Bangor. About 830, under the Norwegian jarl Turgeis, they were plundering Patrick's holy seat of Armagh. Two years later Turgeis sat mocking in its abbot's chair, while his wife, Aud, from the high altar of Clonmacnois declaimed heathen prophecies as a witch-woman from her own Scandinavia. Turgeis went on to make himself lord of northern Ireland and to raid the countryside here and there, in Connacht and in Meath. But at last, in 845, the men of Meath rose up in their wrath, captured him, and drowned him in their Lough Owel, near Mullingar.

From Ireland, Vikings of Vestfold sailed to the west coast of France, also to pillage and occupy the land. In 836 we find them laying waste the monasteries along the Loire from their headquarters on the Isle of Noirmoutier, at the mouth of the river; again and again they raided the helpless Frisian coast. After Louis the Pious was dead and his three sons divided his dominions, with Lothar, the eldest, as emperor in his right, year after year saw Frankish cities in flames. In 845 came the first assault upon Paris. A monk of Saint-Germain-des-Près wrote of "Northmen, most impious, most cruel, blasphemers of God," who hanged one hundred and eleven Frankish prisoners in full sight of the king of France, Charles the

Bald, and swarmed from their ships into Paris on Easter morning to seize its gold. They were urged on, it seems, by the famous Viking, Ragnar Lothbrok; and Frankish annals declare that King Charles paid in gold and silver seven thousand pounds as price for their departure and, as he hoped, for his own peace.

Upon England the evil came at first so quietly that men scarcely recognized it. In the time of that Beorhtric who was king of Wessex from 786 to 802, three Norwegian ships from Hörthaland, the region around Hardanger Fjord, put into shore near Portland in Dorset. Word of this was carried to the king's inspector of customs, a man named Beaduheard of the town of Dorchester twelve miles away, who at once mounted his horse and rode with a few of his men to see these strangers. They must be merchants, he thought, arriving on friendly errand. Yet he could not be sure, and so he ordered them somewhat sharply to get them to the royal manor for questioning. Then and there they killed him and his men.

In 793 England's sacred shrine, the monastery which guarded St. Cuthbert's relics upon the Isle of Lindisfarne off the Northumbrian coast, was sacked and destroyed by Norwegian raiders. Alcuin wrote from his palace school among the Franks a cry of horror and shock: "Some three hundred and fifty years have we and our fathers dwelt in this fair land, and never before has such terror appeared in Britain as now has come upon us from heathen men. We never even dreamed it possible that this should strike us from ships by sea." Of course, he declared, it was the righteous wrath of heaven visiting sinners for their hideous crimes, their unbridled indulgences.

Had not omens of evil lately given Englishmen to fear they knew not what?

The next year Bede's monastery of Jarrow in Durham was plundered. After this, upon English shores there was quiet for forty years. Then in 835 Danish Vikings came across the Channel, and for more lasting attack. That year they overran the Isle of Sheppey, at the mouth of the Thames. In 836 thirty-five of their ships won victory from King Egbert at Carhampton in Somerset. But in 838, the year before his death, he ended his reign happily, by putting to flight both Danes and the Cornishmen who joined them, in that battle of Hingston Down.

Under Ethelwulf the menace grew stronger and more constant, in Wessex as elsewhere. Each year from 840 to 843 the Vikings won their cause; against the men of Dorset; against the men of Lincolnshire, of East Anglia, of Kent; in London and Rochester and Southampton; and a second time at Carhampton, with thirty-five ships, against King Ethelwulf and Somerset men. Then came a victory for Wessex. Not long before Alfred was born, the men of Dorset and the men of Somerset, led by their ealdormen and by their warrior bishop, Ealhstan of Sherborne, fought a Danish army where the river Parret flows into Bridgwater Bay on the west coast of Somerset and with great slaughter drove them to the sea.

CHAPTER TWO

The World OF ALFRED'S BOYHOOD, 849–65

IN THE REIGN of Ethelwulf, Berkshire had at last become permanently part of Wessex. Here, at Wantage, in 849 Alfred was born, on a royal manor of his father's holding, a family estate which long afterward he himself was to leave in legacy to his wife. Beyond it to the north lay the Vale of the White Horse, of fertile meadowland and harvest, and south of it were the Lambourn Downs, the home of wandering sheep. This manor of Lambourn also lay in Alfred's possession when he was king. Nearby ran the ancient Icknield Way, along which men were already traveling a thousand years before Christ, by which perhaps Saxon invaders had first come into Berkshire from their landing on England's east coast, moving on across the Fens of Cambridgeshire and the Chilterns to the Berkshire Downs.

Alfred was the youngest of five children, four sons and a daughter, borne to Ethelwulf by his wife Osburh.

From her they inherited a strain of Jutish blood through her father, Oslac, who as seneschal presided over the hospitality of King Ethelwulf's banquet hall. His descent, and therefore hers, is of twofold interest. It connected her herself with her husband's royal House of Wessex, since Oslac, it would appear, counted among his ancestors that Cerdic who founded the line of West Saxon kings. And, second, among Oslac's forebears is seen at least one of the Jutish nobles who came, probably from Kent, during the sixth century to settle in Hampshire and the Isle of Wight.

Around Alfred as a little child men and women talked constantly of the Viking invaders. He was hardly two years old when word came that King Ethelwulf's eldest son, Athelstan, who seems to have been born of a union previous to the marriage with Osburh and was now ruling under his father the four regions of Kent, Essex, Sussex, and Surrey, had won a great victory at sea over the Danes off Sandwich in Kent, had killed very many of their men, had captured nine of their ships and put the rest to flight. About the same time no fewer than three hundred and fifty Viking ships had appeared at the mouth of the Thames. These ships had not yet reached the awesome size and array which they were to assume later on. But even now the ships of the leaders surely struck terror into southeastern England by their high sterns ending in a dragon's or in a serpent's head, their four-square sails gaily striped in bright colors, the shields, painted black and yellow, hanging along their sides, their prows, beaked and crested like a bird. And, in any case, the rapid tenfold increase from thirty-five to three hundred and fifty ships, each with from thirteen to twenty benches of rowers on either side, and the sight of these rowers striking the water in regular measure as they came toward the river must have brought the men of Thames-side breathless to the shore.

The Danes landed in Kent and wrought ruin on Canterbury and London. London, as we have seen, was a Mercian city and already had been assaulted with great loss of life nine years before. Wiglaf's successor as king of Mercia, Beorhtwulf, marched promptly to its defense; but he could do nothing, and fled, leaving the invaders to cross the river into Surrey. Somewhere south of the Thames, at an unknown place called "Aclea," their march was stopped. King Ethelwulf, with his second son, Ethelbald, and all his army, fought them long and fiercely and, as the old record puts it, 'made there the greatest slaughter in a heathen host of which we have heard tell unto this present day, and took the victory."

Such tidings made good hearing to those at home. But their joy was more than offset by the fact that the Vikings now, for the first time, had remained all the winter just past, of 850–51, in Kent upon the Isle of Thanet. Men realized now that this menace, after fifteen years of scattered raiding, had at last come to stay.

Two years afterward Mercia's king and his counselors appealed for aid to Ethelwulf against another foe. The Welsh had crossed the border and were ravaging lands of England in return for English assaults of earlier days.

The history of Wales in the ninth century has its own place in our story. Its land was then divided into four great regions: Gwynedd in the northwest, including Anglesey and the wild solitudes of the mountains of Snowdonia; Powys, the central part; Deheubarth, in the south, extending over Ceredigion, Dyfed, Ystrad Tywi, and Brycheiniog; and, fourth, Morgannwg, running down to the southern coast and the Bristol Channel. These years saw much political change in Wales, especially in Gwynedd. In the year 825 its royal line of kings had come to an end through the death of its ruler Hywel. Promptly one Merfyn Frych, Merfyn the Freckled, a noble of slender right in descent but of personal power and ambition, not only won its crown but proceeded further to strengthen his stand by taking as wife Nest, sister of Cyngen, king of Powys. Thus he held his power intact for nineteen years. At his death in 844, five years before the birth of Alfred, it had come to an heir who was to be far more renowned. This was Merfyn's son, Rhodri Mawr, Rhodri the Great, destined to reign until 878 and to rule a kingdom far wider than that which he had inherited.

North Wales was not left unmolested by the Vikings. Its annals tell that in 850 one Cyngen was slain by them; that three years later Anglesey was laid waste by the same "Black Gentiles."

Now, in this year of 853, King Ethelwulf listened to the plea of Mercia, led his army through its land into Wales, wrung promise of tribute from the Welsh, and after Easter sealed his alliance with Mercia by giving his only daughter, Alfred's sister Ethelswith, to Burhred, its king since the preceding year, in a splendid ceremony at his royal manor of Chippenham in Wiltshire. She was only a mere child, for in this royal family she was born next to the youngest, Alfred himself, in line.

2

Perhaps Alfred was present at his little sister's wedding. He was four years old. Perhaps, child though he was, he was even then thinking, half-thrilled, half-afraid, of the summer that lay before him. His father, the king, who by now had long despaired of getting to Rome in the present state of things, decided to send there this youngest son of his that he at least might receive the blessing of the Holy Father.

We are not told exactly what led Ethelwulf to this resolve. We do know that Pope Hadrian the First, at Easter, 781, had blessed and anointed two little sons of Charles the Great: Pepin as king of Italy and Louis as king of Aquitaine. Pepin was four and Louis was three. The pope, too, had made himself godfather to Pepin and regularly afterward addressed Charles as *compater* in his letters. In England itself, Offa, the great ruler of Mercia, had seen his young son, Egfrith, anointed in solemn rite by the church as sharer with himself in Mercia's kingship. Perhaps, with such precedents before him, Ethelwulf desired the same honors for his son.

Yet, at the age of four, Alfred's succession to a crown, in the place of his father or under his father during Ethelwulf's life, rested on nothing but a dream, with three older brothers and their sons in view or in prospect. We know, however, that Alfred was especially dear to his father, and this affection, to a king as devoted to Rome as

Ethelwulf, might well have seemed sufficient reason for his son's reception at the hands of the pope.

News spread very slowly in those times. Men's ears were not smitten hourly by reports of death, disaster, and destruction. Moreover, sickness, injury, death itself, were accepted as necessary, inevitable, as the normal lot of man, whether he journeyed forth or stayed at home. Ethelwulf, apparently, would not have hesitated to send this little boy across a channel infested by pirates, past cities destroyed by fire and still burning, to a land terrified by invasion, even had he been clearly aware of perils on the Continent. Three years before, Rorik the Dane, brother of that Harold the Second who had submitted to baptism under Louis the Pious in return for his aid, had scoured the land of Frisia and the banks of the Rhine and the Lek. The Emperor Lothar could do nothing to stop him and was forced to offer him alliance and to seal it with the gift of Duurstede, a busy and much-frequented Frisian port. But the devastation in Frisia and along the Rhine went on. The monastery of St. Bavo in Ghent was ruined; Beauvais went up in flames; and on Christmas Day, 852, the Emperor Lothar and his brother, Charles the Bald, sat encamped on the Seine, looking across the river to the enemy's massed strength. Nothing, once more, could be done here by the two Frankish rulers. Their men would not rally for battle; instead, they soon drifted away in ignominious retreat. The year of Alfred's journey to Rome, 853, was to find the Vikings also in the region of the Loire, burning Nantes, Angers, Poitiers, and—a sacrilege which horrified all the Christian world—"like a savage hurricane" destroying and plundering in Tours the treasures of the two monasteries of St. Martin, one within the city, the other outside it, at Marmoutier, where one hundred and twenty-six monks were killed.

We do not know by what route Alfred and his large escort "of men, noble and simple," crossed the Channel. Perhaps they traveled by way of Quentavic, near Étaples, on the estuary of the river Canche in the Pas-de-Calais. This was the regular port for travelers from England, but it had been badly damaged by Viking raids in 842 and 844. And, when at last the company reached Rome, they found that Holy City beset by troubles of its own.

3

Much had been happening in Rome of late, and there was much, not only old but new, for Alfred to hear and to see. The pope at this time was Leo the Fourth, who left behind him at his death a notable record of unceasing effort for the care of his city and its Cathedral of St. Peter. Seven years before, during the rule of his predecessor, Sergius the Second, Saracen pirates from Africa and Spain had sailed to the mouth of the Tiber, had landed, and had marched upon Rome. Outside its walls they had fallen upon the Basilica of St. Peter to rob and ransack as they would. Sergius had died before plans for its defense could be realized; but Leo had worked hard and long.

When the boy Alfred arrived, he could see around St. Peter's and its precincts a great wall newly raised, reinforced with strong towers. The Emperor Lothar himself had aided the work; from all sides money had poured in for its making; during four years it had slowly risen.

Only the year before, in 852, Pope Leo had dedicated it, and no doubt the royal pilgrims from Wessex now heard all that had been done.

Escorted by his bishops and priests and lesser clergy, Leo had walked in procession around the great church, now, as all hoped, safe from assault, all of them barefooted, with ashes on their heads, singing litanies and psalms. Three times the procession had stopped, the third time at the Postern Gate which looked toward the quarter known as the "School of the Anglo-Saxons." This lay not far from the Tiber and held inns for pilgrims and the "Church of the Blessed Virgin Mary, where the Divine Mysteries were celebrated for the English who came to Rome and where an Englishman who died there might find burial." Here, as the procession halted, the pope had prayed the Lord that "this City which I, Thy servant, Leo the Fourth, Bishop, have dedicated in new building through Thine aid, which from my name is now called Leonine, may ever remain unharmed and secure." It was the twenty-seventh of June, two days before the Feast of St. Peter and St. Paul. After the procession the pope had sung Mass in his Cathedral and had given gifts to all in the city, whether Roman or stranger. For so he had vowed he would do, if God allowed his intent.

But Alfred had come to Rome that he might be received by the head of his church. Leo the Fourth was no idle dreamer and did not anoint the little boy as one who was to be king. What he did he told in a letter which he now wrote to King Ethelwulf: "Your son Alfred, whom you have sent at this time to the *limina* of the Holy Apostles, I have gladly received, and as my spiritual son

I have girded him with the honor and the outward array of nobility after the manner of consuls at Rome, because he has given himself into my hands."

Doubtless this ceremony lingered in Alfred's imagination as he crossed the Channel homeward. Many years afterward he must have had it in mind when he knighted his young grandson, Athelstan, arrayed him in scarlet cloak and jeweled baldric, and hung from his side a Saxon sword sheathed in gold.

4

Meanwhile Alfred's royal father, Ethelwulf, was at home in Wessex, planning, praying, listening. Soon he had other news from Rome. Cyngen, that king of Powys in north-central Wales, who was uncle of Rhodri the Great, king of Gwynedd, had left his kingdom to seek in the Holy City solace from the vexation of invaders and aggressors, and there in 854 he died. His realm of Powys was at once captured by this nephew, Rhodri, who added its lands to his own of Gwynedd. The men of Powys raised no revolt. No doubt at this moment they were glad to have a strong ruler who might defend them from English assault.

News, and disheartening news, came also this year from Viking quarters. King Horik the Dane, who had befriended St. Anskar in his missionary work and had done much to keep Danish jarls from raiding the Channel coasts, was dead, murdered with all his heirs, except one boy, in a rebellion raised by his nephew, Guthrum. Henceforth the Danish menace, Ethelwulf knew well, would surely not lessen its energy; in all probability it would instead rapidly increase.

The year 855 brought word of two more deaths. July the seventeenth saw that of young Alfred's lately won Father in God, Pope Leo the Fourth, presently enrolled as saint of the church. At the end of September the monastery of Prüm, near Trier in the modern Rhineland of Germany, was chanting requiem for the departed soul of the Frankish emperor, Lothar the First. Sick in body and weary at heart of family quarrels and pirate visitations, he had renounced his crown, divided his realms among his three sons, and retreated to spend his last days in religion. Within a few weeks his body lay in its coffin, tonsured and girded with monastic habit. His eldest son, Louis the Second, now became emperor of the Franks. To the middle son, Lothar the Second, came those lands between France and Germany, the lands of the Rhine, the Moselle, and the Meuse. Now under him and in his name they were made into a newborn entity, destined to play an important part amid medieval intrigue as the state of Lotharingia.

Meanwhile the Danes were still keeping men awake at night on the English coast. All the winter of 854–55 they had remained encamped on the Isle of Sheppey, Kent. Whether King Ethelwulf, like the Emperor Lothar, lost strength for the struggle, or whether he judged that prayer and pilgrimage and consultation with the pope were his best resource in this hour of emergency, we do not know. At all events, sometime during this year of 855 he decided to make his own way to Rome and to take with him on yet a second visit his son Alfred, now six years old.

Perhaps, too, the loss by death of Alfred's mother, Osburh, had strengthened in Ethelwulf's mind the desire for this pilgrimage. Little is told us about this wife of his. But there is one scene in our sources, described to us by Alfred's friend and bishop, Asser, which shows her in a pleasant light. Her youngest son, Alfred, from his earliest years loved to listen to his mother's reading of the old stories told in verse in that Anglo-Saxon which he used every day as his own familiar tongue. Long afterward, when he was a man, he was bitterly vexed that, as he said, he did not himself learn to read until his twelfth year, and he blamed his parents and those who had charge of him for this careless neglect. He added, however, that there were no good teachers in the whole of Wessex when he was growing up, and this we may understand as true of the south of England. Learning and the art of script were still flourishing in the north during the ninth century in spite of Viking battles and siege. In the south, on the other hand, the storming of Canterbury, the constant raids upon the coast, and the permanent presence of Vikings at Thanet and Sheppey were taking their toll of men's energy and of their leisure for books.

But Queen Osburh read the Anglo-Saxon poems in her family. And one day, Asser tells us, she held out to Alfred and his brothers the book in her hands and said, "Whichever of you shall learn to read this book first shall have it for his own." Alfred eagerly asked whether she really meant it. When she answered with a smile and a nod that indeed she did, he took the book from her and went with it to his teacher, such as he was. Apparently the teacher read all its poems to him again and again, until the little boy, five or six years old, knew them by heart. Then he returned to recite them to his mother and triumphantly to carry off his prize.

This story does throw some light upon the lack of education of even royal children at this time and of the absence of educated men even at the Wessex court. Ethelwulf, it is true, held for some while in his service a Frankish secretary, named Felix, versed in Latin and in Saxon language and script. But from him we learn only of his royal master's zeal and generosity toward his church.

This zeal was now proved. Before the king left England for Rome, he gave over, apparently to various individual officers and nobles of his household and administration, estates amounting to one-tenth of his land, estates which in his careful and deliberate planning were eventually to pass into ecclesiastical and monastic ownership, free from all obligation of tax except the three usual contributions to public funds for the support of the national army and for the building of fortresses and of bridges over streams and rivers.

On his way to Rome the king of Wessex was welcomed in France with all royal honor by Charles the Bald, king of the Franks in the west, who discussed with him matters of deep interest for their future friendship and gave him escort to the frontier. Ethelwulf lingered nearly a year in the Holy City, asking counsel of the pope, visiting many shrines, and offering to the Church of St. Peter magnificent gifts of Saxon workmanship which he had brought from England. These are duly described in the *Book of the Popes:* a crown, two basins and two little statues, all of the purest gold; a sword, bound with gold; four hanging disks of silver, covered with gold, to be used as support for sanctuary lights; a silk dalmatic, with stripe woven in gold thread; an alb of white silk, embroidered in gold; two curtains of texture rich and shining. The king also gave presents of money of gold and silver to bishops, priests, deacons, lesser clerics, and secular nobles of Rome. Lastly, he scattered small pieces of silver among its people in general, at the desire of the pope.

The pope was now Benedict the Third. Very possibly Ethelwulf and his son Alfred were already in the Holy City at the time of the troubles which followed Benedict's election in the summer of 855. A conspiracy had risen to oppose this candidate. High dignities, including envoys of the Emperor Louis, clamored for the well-known cardinal-priest Anastasius, who under Leo the Fourth had been excommunicated as traitor to the Holy See. For three days tumult raged in Rome, where, it was said, "things were done which no Saracen would think of doing." Probably matters in tradition were to appear worse than the reality. We read, however, of images broken in St. Peter's, of the pope-elect Benedict, stripped of his vestments, beaten, and imprisoned. Finally, order was restored. A multitude of Rome's people, crowding into the Lateran, called for Benedict as pope, a triduum of fast and prayer was held, the rebels submitted, and Benedict was consecrated, either on the last Sunday in September or the first in October.

5

The winter of 855–56 was severe, and plague carried off many in Europe. Ethelwulf and his son, in the spring or early summer of 856, came to stay a second time in France, on their way home, as guests of its king. There was once again plenty of matter for discussion. Charles the Bald, like Ethelwulf, was passionately devoted to his church and as keen on theological argument as his grandfather, Charles the Great, had been. Political troubles, however, were harassing him more and more. For years Brittany had been a source of trouble, fighting to maintain its independence. Aquitaine, which had sworn loyalty seven years before, had since then been constantly in revolt and now in 856 was asking aid of Louis, ruler of Germany; only delay on Germany's part drove the men of Aquitaine to make peace with Charles and accept his will. In the middle of August the Viking Danes were once more on the Seine, burning monasteries and castles on either bank and preparing to remain for the winter. The Saracens had worked ruin in Naples. The church of France was rent by ecclesiastical turmoil and by theological strife. And everywhere men were talking about Charles the Bald's nephew, the young Lothar who held that new kingdom of Lotharingia.

Lothar had been forced by his father and the nobles of France into a marriage which he hated and now was longing to break. For years he had been devoted to a mistress named Waldrada; and he was trying to induce church and state to allow him to repudiate his wife, Theutberga, and to make Waldrada his lawful queen.

The storm raised by this struggle was to last fourteen years and end only upon Lothar's death: "the source of ruin," as a Frankish record described it, "not only of himself but of all his realm."

In these circumstances it was natural that Charles the Bald, king of France, should be glad to ally himself firmly with the king of Wessex in England and that both rulers should be united in facing the common threatening of pirate raids. Accordingly, it was announced in July that Ethelwulf, whose wife Osburh had died, we do not know when, was to marry the daughter of Charles, Judith by name. No reason other than that of political expediency is suggested for this union of a devout king, a ruler now for seventeen years and the father of six children, with a young girl, little more than a child. The nuptials were solemnly celebrated on the first of October, 856, in the royal castle at Verberie-sur-Oise, near the Forest of Compiègne, by the leading prelate of France, Hincmar, archbishop of Reims.

The choice of officiant for the ceremony was natural. It was Hincmar who constantly upheld the cause of Charles the Bald; who was to crown him in 869 as king of Lotharingia, after the death of that unhappy nephew, Lothar; who was to denounce in words which rang throughout France Lothar's faithlessness to his marriage vows; who was holding captive in his own diocese the young Gottschalk, condemned by the church for heresy; who fought the long and bitter theological battle raging in France against predestination, both to good and to evil; who upheld with zeal the priestly character of a king and, with still greater zeal, the duty of a king to obey in humility and faithfulness the head of God's church on earth.

It was he, then, who now not only blessed young Judith as a wedded wife but anointed and crowned her as a queen, in her own dignity as consort of King Ethelwulf of Wessex—a crowning at that time not of tradition or of usage for a king's consort even in Judith's own France. We still have in its original wording the Latin ritual chanted over her at Verberie by the archbishop. He was now about fifty years old, and Ethelwulf was, more or less, of the same age:

The Lord crown thee with glory and honour and place upon thy head the precious stones of the Spirit; that whatsoever is here of token in the sheen of gold and the varied sparkling of jewels, may ever shine forth in thee and in thy doings: Which thing may He Himself vouchsafe to grant, to Whom is honour and glory for all ages to come, Amen.

Bless, O Lord, this Thy servant: Thou Who from all time dost rule the realms of Kings. Amen.

One would like to have seen young Alfred, at the age of six, watching and listening—as presumably he did—during this splendid ceremony which gave him in place of Queen Osburh a stepmother thirteen years old.

The marriage was to bear unwelcome harvest. When Ethelwulf at last, in 856, after a year's absence returned home to Wessex, many men of his land received him with joy. His nobles, indeed, were surprised to see Judith, crowned in France, sitting at his side as queen, contrary to Wessex custom. Men of Wessex had not forgotten the story of their King Beorhtric's death at the hands of Eadburh, his Mercian wife. Yet this was not the worst.

Either before or during Ethelwulf's stay on the Continent, his eldest son, Athelstan, had died. To the next son in age, Ethelbald, had doubtless fallen the fulfilling of many royal functions in Wessex. Now the king's long absence, together with outraged feeling against this new and strange marriage of his, and, we may suppose, with ambition, also, on the part of Ethelbald, was moving this son to aim at permanent possession of his father's crown.

Ethelbald was a man of very different character from his father. He was determined and unscrupulous; but he, too, had friends. He was supported by a following under two Wessex leaders: the warlike Ealhstan, bishop of Sherborne, and Eanwulf, ealdorman of Somersetshire. These men had at first plotted to keep Ethelwulf from even setting foot again in his kingdom; but they were foiled in this by the loyalty of Wessex lords and officials at large.

Matters, however, became daily more serious. Soon civil war was threatening. The people, hurrying to the support of their king, were ready to rise and drive Ethelbald and his party into exile. Then Ethelwulf, to save his country, yielded his right. He gave over to Ethelbald the rule of Wessex proper and retired to govern as underking the four regions formerly administered by his eldest son, Athelstan: Kent, Essex, Sussex, and Surrey. It was an act in keeping with his character; and here his wife Judith was freely accorded the honor due to a queen.

Some two years later Ethelwulf was dead. These years in the southeast of England were darkened by news from the Frankish kingdom of his father-in-law, Charles the Bald. There the Viking pirates on the Seine under Björn Ironside, held in tradition as another son of Ragnar Lothbrok, once more set Paris on fire and worked havoc among its churches, one after another. Only four were said to have remained unharmed. Paschasius Radbert, the learned monk of Corbie, near Amiens, turned from his study of the *Lamentations* of Jeremiah to write lament for his own world in words which recall Alcuin's horror over ruined Lindisfarne:

The kings of the earth, and all the inhabitants of the world, would not have believed that the adversary and the enemy should have entered into the gates of Jerusalem:

"Who would believe," Paschasius wrote, "which among us could have imagined, that that could happen which we have seen and wept, that the enemy should enter our own Paris and burn the churches of Christ on its river's shore?"

In 858, the year of Ethelwulf's death, Charles, driven by necessity, marched to besiege Viking headquarters on the Isle of Oissel in the Seine, near Mantes; but he was forced to abandon the blockade when his brother, Louis the German, seized this opportune moment to attack him. It was Hincmar who rallied the bishops of France to the cause of their King Charles and turned the evil tide.

Ethelwulf was buried at Winchester. In his will he directed that one poor man, native or stranger, should be given allowance, of food and clothing, for every ten hides of the royal estates that were not barren land and that this direction should stand in permanence. To Rome he left an annual revenue of three hundred mancuses, gold coins, each equal in value to thirty silver pennies, or somewhat more than the current price of an ox. Of these three hundred mancuses, two hundred were to be used in buying oil for lamps in honor of St. Peter and St. Paul at Rome, and one hundred were left to the pope to use every year at his discretion. A ring of gold, bearing Ethelwulf's name and the heraldic device of two birds, and also one inscribed with the name of Alfred's sister Ethelswith, wife of King Burhred of Mercia, are still to be seen in the British Museum.

Ethelbald, Alfred's eldest surviving brother, was now, in 858, ruler of Wessex in full right. The rule of the four regions of the southeast passed to the next brother, Ethelbert. Ethelbald's reign was brief; but it was marked by an event described in record of this ninth century as "contrary to the law of God and the honor of Christendom, nay, contrary to all *heathen* use." The king took as wife his, and Alfred's, own stepmother, the young widow, Judith, even now only fifteen years of age. All men in England, we are told, were horrified.

The marriage lasted only two years or a little more. In 860 Ethelbald died and was buried at Sherborne, in Dorset. Then Alfred's third brother, Ethelbert, as king united under his rule all the lands of Wessex, both in the west and in the southeast. Judith, twice a widow at eighteen, sold all her possessions in England and returned to France, where her father kept her under close guard in his castle at Senlis, hoping that she might soon be decently and honorably settled in marriage. He had other matters to think about. The Vikings were still on the Seine, and he was pondering all means in his power to drive them thence.

Her father's troubles did not worry young Judith

overmuch. She was finding consolation for her long dull hours at Senlis in visits from the handsome and energetic Baldwin "Iron-Arm," destined to be the first count of Flanders. Her brother, Louis the Stammerer, secretly gave her aid; and soon all France was scandalized by the news that Baldwin and this princess and former queen had eloped. In his rage King Charles incited the bishops of France to excommunicate his daughter's lover. Had not Gregory the Great declared that he who steals a widow for wife is anathema? And was not he himself, the king of France, at this very moment uniting with his archbishop, Hincmar of Reims, in defense of a marriage sealed by the church, in defense of the unhappy Theutberga, the wife of that immoral nephew of his, Lothar of Lotharingia? And had not the guilty couple, his daughter and her paramour, fled for refuge to this very Lothar himself?

But Baldwin fled also to an abler source of help. He went to Rome and laid his cause before the pope, now the great Nicholas the First. Nicholas listened with sympathy. He wrote to the wrathful Charles that these two young people sincerely loved each other and that it would be an act of mercy to forgive them. An act of wisdom, as well. It would not do, the pope pointed out, to drive young Baldwin by this wrath into alliance with those enemies of all good, the Viking robbers.

Letter after letter followed, to Charles, to his queen, Ermentrude, to the bishops of France; and at last Hincmar, however unwilling, was able to write to the pope that his wish had been in some part fulfilled: "When, Your Holiness, I had received with all reverence your letter and had read it to my fellow-bishops, we pleaded for Judith with her father and her mother and told them of your prayers. And so our Lord King Charles allowed the two to be married at Auxerre according to civil law, and he honored Baldwin, as you had asked of him. But he would not attend the ceremony."

In the meantime Danish Vikings were still busy in France, both on the river Seine and, under a leader named Weland, on the river Somme. Charles, still trying in vain to drive them out, resorted to bribery, in the hope of dividing one camp against the other. He offered to the Danes on the Somme three thousand pounds of silver, carefully weighed, which he proposed to exact from the revenues of the church and the pockets of his people, if these Danes would attack the encampment on the Seine. The amount, however, proved to be greater than Charles could raise, press and drive as he might. The Vikings on the Somme grew weary of waiting, withdrew the hostages through whom they had pledged their bargain, and went off across the Channel to plunder England. Early in this reign of Ethelbert they fell upon Winchester in force, but they were driven off after sharp fighting by the ealdormen of Hampshire and Berkshire.

For some years there now was peace, until in the summer of 865 Thanet was again occupied by Danes who gave no sign of retreating. At length the men of Kent bargained with them for safe living in return for money payments; and the invaders accepted the promise of money. Then, protected by this agreement, when all had settled down in quiet, they sallied out by night and laid waste all eastern Kent.

6

During these years of Ethelbert's reign, five in all, Alfred was growing from a boy of eleven into a lad of sixteen. He was spending his days in the royal manors of Wessex, at Wantage and Chippenham, at Wilton and Winchester. He was visiting, we may suppose, his sister, Queen Ethelswith, in Mercia, riding along the old Roman roads. With other boys he ran and wrestled. He delighted in the mornings when the king, his brother, and the nobles of the court hunted in Selwood Forest the deer, the wolf, and the wild boar. As he grew older, he joined them in their sport and, we are told, loved it. On the royal lands he saw men plowing, sowing, reaping, tending the gardens where grew the herbs for the healing of the sick, for the savoring of food; he talked with the bailiffs and seneschals; in the women's bower he watched curiously the maids who spun and wove. He wore day by day a short belted tunic and carried, like all boys, a knife for many needs; on high days of holiday he put on a cloak of red or purple or blue, fastened by a brooch made of gold or silver and inset with enamel and jewels in the beautiful Frankish and Anglo-Saxon work of early medieval days. In the afternoons he sat at dinner in the king's great hall, where the log fire leaped on the hearth and the torches and candles threw shadows on the walls, and watched the king's nobles and warriors drinking mead and ale from their horns and on feast days wine from the wassail bowl. He heard them talk of pirate raids, of plague and murder, of the darkening of the sun and the moon, of storms and rushing floods. Now and then he listened eagerly to stories of heathen gods, of dragons and witches, of giants and elves, of brave soldiers and their deeds in battle. Sometimes wandering minstrels would arrive and would sing to the harp their tales of heroes of an older land.

He learned, too, his lessons, and now he could himself read his books in Anglo-Saxon. He knew very little Latin at this time; but now and again in curiosity he would pore over the illuminated Latin texts which visitors to the court brought from Canterbury, from the north of England, from Irish monasteries. Something he knew of his family's royal standing. On coins he saw the names of his father and brothers; envoys were always arriving; now and then, when he was old enough, he was called to give his witness to a royal deed of grant, written on parchment by the king's scribe.

Above all, he was taught the meaning of his Christian faith. Day after day he heard Mass in the royal chapel and often, probably, listened to its Offices of the Day. He knew the splendor of great feasts, spiritual and social rejoicing, as at Yuletide and Easter, and felt, too, the strait living of Lent, when high feasting gave way to meager fare of herrings and eels. Sometimes, no doubt, he listened to the ritual of the church at Sherborne and saw its bishop, Ealhstan, who was always talking with the king on the business of war. Sometimes he must have talked with Swithhun, who was his father's counselor in the ways of religion, had taught his father, Ethelwulf, as a boy, and was bishop of Winchester from the time that Alfred was three years old. It was he, men believed, who had inspired Ethelwulf to give the tenth of his land to God.

Many familiar stories were told of Swithhun's humility and of the power of his prayer with heaven. Once, men said, he was standing on a bridge in Winchester when his eye fell upon a woman crossing it on her way to market. She had on her arm a basket of eggs, and, as he looked, she stumbled, her eggs rolled out, and every one of them was broken. Immediately he went up to her and saw that she was old and miserably clad and that tears were running down her face. He lifted his hand, so the story went, made the sign of the cross, and lo! the eggs lay on the street whole, in their unbroken shells once more. Like holy Aidan long before him, this bishop Swithhun would not ride on horseback about his great diocese but went on foot, and did it at night lest men should mock or taunt him for his humility. Solitude and simple living were alike dear to his heart. He died when Alfred was twelve or thirteen, and left word that he be buried outside his cathedral, "beneath the feet of passers-by and the rain dripping from the eaves."

The quiet which marked much of Ethelbert's reign was the quiet before the breaking of the storm. In 865 he, too, died and was buried beside his brother Ethelbald at Sherborne. Then Alfred's last remaining brother, Ethelred, came to the throne of Wessex; and Alfred at the age of sixteen turned to face with him years of assault and battle such as they had never known or dreamed could come in their time upon their land.

CHAPTER THREE

Alfred AND HIS BROTHER, KING ETHELRED, 865–71

TWO EVENTS of great importance mark the autumn of this year 865. The first was the rise of Alfred to a share in kingly power. Ethelred, for all his youth, was a ruler and a soldier of resolute mind and will, determined to face with all his strength whatever lay before him and his country. Although he was as loyal and devoted to his church as his father, Ethelwulf, had been, for him at this time the duty of a Christian ruler of Wessex was to stand and fight for its defense. In this he was a king of ideal character in the mind of his younger brother, Alfred, now coming forward for the first time to take his own place in councils of war and peace. Ethelred gladly encouraged him, and Alfred quickly entered upon this new co-operation. For six years we shall find him standing side by side with the king of Wessex as his second in command—*secundarius*, as Asser describes him in the Latin *Life*—both in conference and on the field of battle.

Now—and this is the second event—all their united energy was called into action. The Scandinavian invaders had had their fill of scattered raids, of single winters spent in England. Suddenly they descended in multitude, determined to conquer and to occupy this English land, to dwell and to settle in permanence with their families and kinsmen, as they had done on the Scottish islands, as they had done within Ireland itself.

In the autumn of 865 two sons of Ragnar Lothbrok sailed to England with a great host of Danes. Their names have come down to us as Halfdan and Ivar the Boneless. Scandinavian legend told that Kraka, the young and lovely bride of Ragnar, had pleaded with her lord on their wedding night that they wait three days for the fulfilment of their marriage. A spell lay upon her, she said. But he would not; and so this, their first child, Ivar, was born with gristle where bones should have been. Yet, when he grew to manhood, he outmatched in cunning all men whom he met.

From their multitude of ships the Danes poured into East Anglia and spent the winter there, gathering arms, buying and stealing horses in vast numbers, so that their men might ride on their way. As time went on, in return for free provisioning they left in peace the English who lived near them and were forced to allow this terror in the land. For a year they drew in what they needed, and then, as summer turned again to autumn, they broke camp and rode northward across Lincolnshire and into Yorkshire. At York they halted their march to seize and occupy the city. It was All Saints' Day, the first of November, 866.

The men of Northumbria were even less ready than the East Anglians to offer any real resistance. Civil strife was dividing their city of York at this very time. From it they had recently driven out Osbert, king of Northumbria for eighteen years, and had given his crown to one Aella, who was not in any way connected with their royal house. Osbert, however, still had some following in Northumbria; and the struggle between the two parties went on vigorously until this coming of the Danes. Then the shock of the capture of their chief city threw both king and ex-king into alliance in a desperate effort to regain it.

The whole winter was given by them to plans and preparation. It was not until the twenty-first of March, in Passiontide, 867, that the men of Northumbria rushed into attack. The Danes were entirely taken by surprise, many of them on or outside the old Roman walls of the city, which in their confidence of security they had not troubled to repair and strengthen. At first they fled within, caught by panic, and pursued by the English. But, once inside, they rallied and fought to the death. So did the English, and their loss was far greater. Both their kings, Osbert and Aella, were killed, with eight Northumbrian nobles. The Danes were left in possession, and set up in Northumbria a king of their own choosing and under their will, though he was English by race, Egbert by name.

The historian of St. Cuthbert of Lindisfarne was to declare afterward that both Osbert and Aella had come upon a fate which they richly deserved. God and his saint had overthrown them in righteous wrath for their theft of houses dedicated in Cuthbert's name. That may be true. But other tradition, from Scandinavian source, concerning King Aella is entirely strange to sober history. *The Saga of Ragnar Lothbrok* told that this Ragnar, the father of the present Danish invaders, Halfdan and Ivar, long before this time had sailed from Denmark to England with only two ships and that these were wrecked by a great storm off the Northumbrian coast. But he and his men came safely to shore with their swords and axes and marched through the countryside, raiding and seizing as they went. Word of this outrage was brought to Aella, who then was king in Northumbria, and he summoned all his fighting men to arms. There was a fierce battle, and at last Ragnar was taken alive. Not one word would he speak when he was brought before the king. Then Aella gave order to throw him into a pit full of snakes, with the command that directly he declared himself as Ragnar he was to be released. Ragnar sat a long while, and not a snake came near him. "Take off his outer coat," said Aella. This coat was his wife's parting gift to Ragnar, and it was charged with magic power. The moment he sat down in the pit without it, snakes writhed and curled over his body from head to foot. "The young boars would snarl," he said, "if they knew how the old one suffers," and with that he died. So, as the legend went, it was to revenge their father's death that the sons of Ragnar now came to war upon King Aella.

2

We return to cold fact and to the Danish invaders, still at York in the autumn of 867. A year had passed since they arrived. The fields of Northumbria had been plundered as far as the river Tyne; its men had yielded to Danish terms of peace; it was time to seek fresh conquest. Now the great host mounted horse and rode southward from York into Mercia, where it settled for the winter at Snotingaham, the present Nottingham. Its men no doubt were posted both on the high cliff overlooking the Trent and down below in the Trent Valley, near the little river Leen. Here they were to come directly into contact with Wessex. The king of Mercia was still Burhred, brother-in-law of Ethelred and Alfred; and in this crisis of invasion he and his nobles again appealed to Wessex for help.

It was 868 when the brothers, Ethelred and Alfred, answered his call; and about this time, either shortly before or soon after their coming into Mercia, another bond between Mercia and Wessex was formed. Alfred, now in his twentieth year, took a bride from Burhred's kingdom. Her name was Ealhswith, and she was of noble rank. Her father was Ethelred Mucill, ealdorman of a part of Mercia described as Gaini, but of unknown location. Her mother, who bore the same name, Eadburh, as King Offa's ill-famed daughter, was also connected with Mercia's royal house.

The wedding was celebrated in Mercia with a great assembly of guests, with feasting prolonged far into the night. But its rejoicing was marred by sudden anxiety. At the height of the merriment Alfred was seized by acute pain, to the consternation of all who were crowding around him. Doctors were summoned, but no one could diagnose the trouble. Some suggested a hitherto unknown kind of fever; others, the casting of the evil eye of witchcraft upon the victim by some jealous guest; others, the malice of Satan, always ready to tempt and to hurt good men.

Those who knew Alfred best declared, mistakenly, that this was another, and a specially sharp, attack of the disorder known as the *ficus*, interpreted in modern medicine as probably hemorrhoids. From this trouble Alfred had suffered intermittently since he was a child. His doctors had prescribed remedies of plant healing. Take roots of burdock, they said, and heat them very hot upon the hearth and knead hard into a cake and apply. But touch not the roots with iron, for that makes for evil. Lay hold, too, upon root of celandine with thy hands (again, dig not with iron), and as thou pullest chant nine times the "Our Father" and, when for the ninth time thou comest to "Deliver us from evil," pull up the root and soak it in water and apply to the patient before a hot fire.

Often Alfred had prayed for relief. Once, so the tale went, when he was in Cornwall with the hounds on holiday, he had turned aside from the hunt to offer his hope to heaven at a Cornish shrine now hidden in the mists of unreliable tradition together with the stories of its dedications, first to "St. Gueriir," then to St. Neot. His prayer, men said, had then at last found its answer, and from that hour, we are told, the old ailment had ceased to worry him.

Now, on this night of rejoicing, another anguish had fallen, no one knew whence or why. Nor do we know its nature. Very possibly, as some authorities suggest, it sprang from bladder trouble, through perhaps inflammation; or kidney colic, caused through the forming of stone. The immediate crisis passed after a while; yet for many years Alfred was seldom without suffering, either in the actual pain of attack or in the fear that illness was again going to descend upon him.

3

The campaign of the men of Wessex in Mercia did not last long. The Danes, protected by those strong walls of Nottingham behind which they had withdrawn, refused battle, and their position could not be forced. There was nothing for Burhred and his advisers to do but to make peace; and for Ethelred and Alfred nothing but to return to Wessex.

The invading host soon broke camp and returned to York, where again they stayed a year, from the autumn of 868 to the autumn of 869. It was probably October of 869 when they rode across Mercia back once more into East Anglia, where they had first landed in 865. By this time they had been four years in England, and they had done as they would. Now they decided to settle for the winter at Thetford, at present a small market town and borough on the border line between Norfolk and Suffolk, partly within each. They had been settled there only a short while when they came up against the king of East Anglia, Edmund.

This is the St. Edmund, king and martyr, so well known to English churches. Legend, gradually growing from the tenth until the fourteenth century, was to weave many stories around his boyhood and his death. It was to tell how in this ninth century a certain Offa, who had nothing to do with the famous king of Mercia in the century before, but who was king of East Anglia, troubled in mind because he had no son to succeed him, decided to lay his desire before the Lord as pilgrim in the Holy Land. On his way he passed through Saxony and was welcomed there by its king—we are even given the king's name, Alkmund. Alkmund had two young sons, Edwold and Edmund. Edmund, born in Nuremberg, so won the heart of King Offa that then and there he longed to make the boy his adopted son and heir. The father consented. Offa went on to the Holy Land, died before he could reach home again, and in his last hours ordered his messengers to carry word to Alkmund and to request fulfilment of the promise. It was fulfilled after some natural reluctance; and Edmund landed in East Anglia at a point of land called Maiden's Bower, near Hunstanton. Ever afterward he loved Hunstanton and built himself a dwelling there for his leisure hours. From 855, at the age of fifteen, he was king of East Anglia, accepted and honored by nobles and people alike.

So far we are gleaning most of our story of Edmund from one Gaufridus de Fontibus, who was probably a priest at Thetford in the twelfth century, perhaps in a community of St. Edmund. The story of the death of the king had already been made into an elaborate narrative by Abbo, monk of Fleury-sur-Loire in the tenth century, well over a hundred years after Edmund had died. Abbo, in addition to hearsay, had his own source of information. St. Dunstan of Canterbury gave him some details and in his turn declared he had received them from a very, very old man who had been serving as armor-bearer to King Edmund himself on the very day of his death.

Abbo tells us, then, that Ivar the Boneless invaded East Anglia with his army and, after ravaging and burning its farms and fields, sent a messenger to its king to demand that Edmund yield to him a considerable part of East Anglia's wealth and reign henceforth under Ivar's own overlordship. The young ruler sent back defiance. A Christian king, he declared, had no such love of this life on earth that he would submit to a pagan lord.

Edmund was at that time in his manor of Hoxne, near Eye in Suffolk, and the messenger had scarcely left it when he met Ivar, eagerly coming up with a large force of his Danes. The reply so infuriated him that he sent his men hurrying to seize Edmund. At once in the open field his captive was bound, beaten, mocked, fastened to a tree, and made "another St. Sebastian" by the shooting of many arrows into his body. Finally, his head was struck off and buried deep in a wood nearby. The body was left lying in the field where he had died. The king's men, when they heard of the tragedy, recovered this and, guided by a voice which cried "Here! Here!" searched until they found the head. It was lying between the paws of a huge wolf, which willingly gave up its charge to these Christian and devoted followers of the king and trotted behind the procession as it bore the sacred relics home. These were eventually laid to rest at Beodrices-Weorth in Suffolk, known later as Bury St. Edmunds, St. Edmund's Town.

This is the legend. The truth, or probable truth, so far as it can be accepted on reliable evidence, is very briefly told. King Edmund with his men of East Anglia met and fought the Danish invaders under Ivar in the autumn of

869. The Danes defeated them, killed their king, and raided their country. Indirect evidence—the facts that within a short while Edmund was revered far and wide as a worker of miracles, that his shrine in Suffolk was thronged by pilgrims, that he was enrolled in the calendars of the church as king, saint, and martyr, to be honored on the twentieth of November, held in tradition as the day of his death—this evidence makes it more than probable that Ivar took the king prisoner and then deliberately put him to death because he would not consent to yield either his Christian faith or his kingdom to foreign, pagan, pirate control.

Throughout the Middle Ages St. Edmund's Day was observed. It is still observed, still recorded in the calendars of the Anglican church; and over sixty churches in England are dedicated in his name. That he came from Old Saxon ancestry and that his family had originally come from the Continent may also in reason be held true, as this is told on the authority of Abbo and, very probably, from an earlier source.

4

For a year, from 869 to 870, the Danish invaders lived on the harvests and farms of East Anglia. December, 870, found them again on the march, making their way into Wessex itself, to Reading in Berkshire, the shire of Alfred's birth. Ivar the Boneless is no longer found as leader. He had gone off to Ireland, to rule the Vikings settled there, and there he died some three years later. The Danes, now under the general command of Halfdan, brother of Ivar, pitched their camp east of the royal manor of Reading, between its two rivers, the Thames and the Kennet, and gave three days to building a strong rampart around it. On the third day, while the work was still unfinished, two Danish jarls—one of them named Sidroc—rode out with a party through fields and copses to seize and carry off cattle and horses and other necessary supplies from Berkshire land. The ground was difficult and slippery, for it was now the end of December; and they did not know the countryside. At Englefield, where a village now stands with its Tudor manor house some six miles west of Reading along the course of the Kennet, they were met by Ethelwulf, ealdorman of Berkshire. The men with him were not many, but they were at home among these thickets and meadows. They put the Danes to flight and killed the jarl Sidroc.

Four days afterward, in the first week of January, King Ethelred and his second in command, Alfred, arrived for action, bringing to Reading their main army of Wessex men. Battle followed at once, near the camp of the Danes. The men of Wessex cut down all whom they found outside its rampart; but the Danes rushed out from its gates to fall upon the attackers. At last the enemy drove off Ethelred's attack; and now among its dead the West Country grieved over that bold fighter, Ealdorman Ethelwulf.

A defeat at the moment of arrival was in any case disheartening. The next four days were spent by the king and his brother in restoring morale and in sharpening their battle array. About the eighth of January they marched out with their full force of men to the high ridgeway which runs across the Berkshire Downs. The name of these Downs in old record is given as Ashdown, but where on Ashdown Ethelred's army met the Danes we do not know. The White Horse, cut in the turf on the slope of the Downs at Uffington, the Horse which has so often been held to commemorate a victory gained near its very site by Alfred, goes back, we may believe, far beyond the time of Alfred, even as far as the Early Iron Age. Probably it has lain here since the first century B.C., perhaps made by the hands of the immigrants from the Continent, the Belgae, who in that age were bringing their feeling for art and their vigor of craftsmanship across the Channel to Wessex.

> *Before the gods that made the gods*
> *Had seen their sunrise pass,*
> *The White Horse of the White Horse Vale*
> *Was cut out of the grass.*

The Danes were drawn up in two divisions, one commanded by two kings, Bagsecg and Halfdan, the son of Ragnar Lothbrok, the other by the many jarls who were in their army. To meet this formation, Ethelred divided his own ranks into two forces. He himself led the one facing the division of the Danish kings and gave to Alfred the charge of the one which faced the jarls. It was morning, and the Danes were calling for battle. Alfred, at the head of his division, was impatiently looking for the signal to rush forward. King Ethelred did not appear. Word came that he was in his tent; it was the hour for Mass. To the messenger sent to summon him he made sharp answer. Never so long as he lived would he leave the altar before the priest had ended the holy rite or forsake the service of God for the service of man. Alfred for a while hesitated; he was only second in command. But soon he saw that battle would be fought, with the leaders or without them. Quickly he took sole responsibility and gave the signal to advance. Ethelred was soon seen rushing from his tent. One wonders whether the priest, hearing the clamor, omitted his *Placeat tibi.*

The enemy had the advantage of position, high along the ridge that crossed the Downs. From there they could hurl themselves swiftly in heavy force against the English below them on the slope, which was of chalk, overgrown with grass and doubtless treacherous for footing in midwinter. Halfway up stood one lone thorn tree, stunted by the sharp winds. Around this thorn the battle swayed up and down until night came on. Then the Danes slowly yielded ground and were finally driven away. Their loss was heavy, and we have the names of five of their jarls left dead upon the hill. They fled far and wide in the darkness, pursued by the Wessex men, until with the coming of dawn those who could gained the safety of their camp at Reading.

5

Wessex enjoyed this encouragement but a short while. In another two weeks' time, about January the twenty-second, Ethelred and Alfred were fighting these same invaders some fourteen miles away from Reading. From the base camp there, which had been left under guard, the Danes had quietly crept out, perhaps under cover of night and in separate companies. When the English caught up with them, they were about two miles from Basingstoke, in Hampshire, and strongly intrenched.

Somewhere near the village of Old Basing, among the meadows of the river Loddon, Ethelred yielded to the temptation to try to rush upon their firm position from this marshy ground. The attempt failed, and the Danes "took a victory without spoil."

Nothing is told us of the next two months. Then, in mid-Lent, toward the end of March, probably on the twenty-second, Ethelred and Alfred again renewed the battle in a place called "Meretun," a name that has called out much argument but seems most reasonably to belong to Marten, a village about eight miles southeast of Marlborough in Wiltshire and readily approached by the great ridgeway from Basingstoke. Once more the enemy were marshaled in two divisions, and at first the men of Wessex drove both of these into retreat. All day long they pressed forward their advantage, while very many fell on either side. Among these, on the English side, was Heahmund, who had followed Ealhstan as bishop of Sherborne and, like Ealhstan, readily exchanged his pastoral staff for a battle-ax when his country went to war. Suddenly, as evening was coming on, the English again yielded the field, and the Danes held it in victory.

Upon the heels of this disaster came almost at once the news that another great host of Danish invaders had crossed the Channel, from their base on the Continent, to fight in the campaign of the coming summer. They joined the Danish camp at Reading. Hardly had this been heard when, about the twenty-third of April, in Eastertide, messengers carried through Wessex towns and villages word that King Ethelred was dead. Perhaps he had been gravely wounded in the battle at Marten, and this, indeed, may have caused the sudden retreat of his men on that day. Perhaps exposure on the Downs to the cold winds and rain of early spring had brought sickness to a body weary with exertion and to a mind strained by constant watching and anxiety. He was young, but at least two of his elder brothers had died in their youth.

Alfred, now in his twenty-second year, knew himself called to face alone this redoubled host of Danish Vikings encamped on Wessex land and, as king of Wessex, to lead, defend, and save his people through his own solitary initiative and power.

CHAPTER FOUR

King Alfred AND THE GREAT WAR AGAINST THE DANES, 871–86

ETHELRED HAD LEFT two sons at his death, Ethelhelm and Ethelwold, but they were too young to rule in these dangerous years. All the people of Wessex, counselors and officials, men of the army and of the land, alike welcomed Alfred as king. So widely had he won admiration during his brother's reign, both in council and on the field of battle, that his friends declared the crown might have been his by general acclaim even during Ethelred's life, had he been willing to receive it. As for the new king himself, the sudden descent of this responsibility seems for several weeks almost to have numbed his will and energy. It had been hard enough to hold Wessex against the Danes while his brother could share the burden with him. How was he to shoulder it alone?

Nothing is told us of a ceremony of coronation. This does not mean that it did not take place. It suggests instead that this year of 871 was so full of anxiety and crisis that men had little time or heart for ritual, pageant, and feasting. They may have remembered, too, the solemn blessing which Pope Leo the Fourth had given Alfred as a little boy of four, an act which to many now seemed as an anointing to kingship in itself.

Soon sheer necessity called Alfred into action. Ethelred was buried at Wimborne Abbey in Dorsetshire, where doubtless he had died. An army of Wessex men was keeping watch over the base camp of the Danes at Reading; but, partly to do honor to their dead king, partly to act as escort to King Alfred, a detachment had gone with him to Wimborne for the funeral rites. The Danes naturally seized this propitious chance for attack; and there was a battle. It was spirited but short. The men of Wessex before long were forced to give way through lack of numbers, and from Reading the Danes once more raided Berkshire far and wide.

No fewer than nine battles were fought by Wessex during this one year; yet the English did not lose heart. Sallies and assaults were made by them without number, here and there, by day and by night, and not without some success. The Danes lost one of their kings and nine jarls, and, declared Asser, who heard the story from Alfred himself, "how many men God alone knows." The king constantly rode with his Wessex army, as did his ealdormen and his other lords, secular and spiritual. His was truly a fyrd, a Wessex army of Wessex freemen, nobles and ceorls, fighting for their land and people against these intruders from without.

Then came a time when the unequal struggle could not be maintained. Alfred's men were weary, sick, or dead; their farms were destroyed, their herds driven off in plunder. Not even the king could urge them to fresh effort. There were not enough of them, strong and eager, to make victory into a thing to be assured. Alfred talked long and earnestly with his counselors. Then he made offer of peace to the invaders and paid them money, on condition that they should abandon their camp at Reading and depart from Wessex land. This they did, and for four years, from 871 to 875, Wessex had some measure of quiet.

2

Its gain was loss for Mercia, and especially for Burhred, Mercia's ruler. The great Danish host, like a swarm of locusts, moved on to London, still a Mercian town, and stayed there through the winter until the spring or early summer of 872. Then they rode north again to Northumbria.

There was trouble that year in Northumbria. Its people had risen in revolt against that man of their own nation, Egbert, whom the Danes had set up as king under Danish control. Egbert had been driven from his kingdom, and with him Wulfhere, archbishop of York. Both men fled to the hospitality of Burhred in Mercia. Now the invaders stayed a brief while in Northumbria, trying to restore order; but at the moment they could do little, and, as the winter was almost at hand, they moved on to settle at Torksey, in Lindsey.

By Lindsey we may already at this time understand the present Parts of Lindsey in Lincolnshire. It was closely linked with Mercia and looked to Mercian kings for support. The town of Torksey had a double advantage for the Danes through possession of two waterways. It stood at the junction of the river Trent with the ancient canal, the Fossdyke, in use long ages before this ninth century. A village of Torksey still stands to the north of the Fossdyke.

Here the Danes stayed during the winter, spring, and summer of 872–73 in order to glean what they could still gather after their previous plundering. Then once more their hungry spirit carried them away. First, they exacted from their unwilling hosts a price for peace, and then in the autumn of 873 they encamped for yet another winter on Mercian soil, at Repton, Derbyshire, eight miles southwest of Derby and about a mile from the Trent.

At last the sight of widespread destruction and the steady occupying of his country was too much for Burhred, king of Mercia. For three years, since 871, the Danes had been at work on fields and towns, on churches and monasteries over which he held charge of protection, from London to Lindsey, from Lindsey to Repton. Twice in days past, as we have seen, he had appealed to Wessex; but for this he had now no heart. In 874 he suddenly abandoned his kingdom and fled for peace and a quiet life in Rome.

In Rome he was well known. Only this very year he had received a letter from the pope, now John the Eighth. "Immorality, we hear, is rife among you in England," the pope had written. "We hear that your men dare to enter into marriage with nuns and women dedicated to God, and women, too, of their own kindred, contrary to the ruling of holy Gregory. This is indeed a crime, a grievous offense. Herewith by these letters of our Apostolate we bid that all under your authority, cleric and lay, flee such sin for the future, and do meet penance for the past. If this responsibility be hard for you in your present straits, inform our Paternity by letter, that we may summon to the Holy See those who are caught in the toils of action so impious."

This letter may well have added the last drop to Burhred's cup of despair. He was a broken man when he arrived in Rome, and his days there were soon ended. He was buried in that Church of Our Lady built for English pilgrims in the Anglo-Saxon quarter of the city. His wife, Alfred's sister Ethelswith, apparently stayed in England. We read that she died fourteen years later, on a visit to Rome, and was buried in Pavia.

3

The kingdom of Mercia was now at the complete mercy of the Danes. They did not, however, take it entirely for their own. They gave its rule to one of Burhred's nobles, named Ceolwulf, and it remained, at least nominally, in English hands. But Ceolwulf is inscribed for all time in Anglo-Saxon record as "a thane without sense." The conquerors demanded, and he solemnly swore, that he would do as they desired in all things and give back his rule to them whensoever they should require it. This was tragic news for Alfred, Burhred's brother-in-law and fellow-king.

There was more to come, and worse. In the same year of 874 the Danish host in England entered upon new and terrifying measures. It divided into two great forces. One of these, under Halfdan, son of Ragnar Lothbrok, marched northward to achieve finally Danish occupation of Northumbria, to harry afresh that often-harried land, to ride frequently on raids against the Picts beyond the Forth and the British around the Clyde. The puppet-king Egbert, set up by the Danes, was now dead; and the English of Northumbria were living in restless discontent under his successor, Ricsige. Wulfhere, archbishop of York, had been recalled to his see.

The coming of Halfdan quickly made itself felt. The terror of his presence held York in its grasp, then spread to the towns, villages, and moors of the north. Soon it reached Lindisfarne, the sanctuary of St. Cuthbert on the Northumbrian coast, which had already been destroyed some eighty years before. Ever since he had died, in 687, Cuthbert had been revered above all among English saints; and, if we may believe tradition, this reverence was deeply shared by Alfred himself. Far away in the southwest as he was, he must have felt the fear which now came upon Lindisfarne's monks and their bishop, Eardulf.

In 793 the relics of the saint had been left unharmed amid the ruin of his monastery. Who knew whether they would remain in the present storm? Lindisfarne had often heard repeated those words which Cuthbert had said in his last hours to Herefrith, its abbot of that time, when his monks had begged that the body of this, their father and bishop, might be buried in their church:

This you must know and keep in mind, that if necessity compel you to choose one of two evils, I would far rather that you take my bones out from their grave and depart hence, carrying them with you as you go. God will take thought for you wheresoever you shall tarry to dwell. Far better is this than that for any cause you should consent to iniquity and bow your necks to the yoke of unbelievers.

So now the monks of Lindisfarne took up the holy relics. It was 875 when their little company slowly at low tide crossed the sands which lie between Lindisfarne and the mainland. There it broke up. Eardulf knew that it would be long before his monks would again have a settled home. He bade the older go their different ways and delivered the sacred burden to his younger clergy, to carry wheresoever they could find shelter and safekeeping for it. Then he, as their bishop, and Eadred, their abbot, took their places at the head of the line, and it started forth. For seven years the body of St. Cuthbert was carried here and there in its wanderings, and always the monks who bore it kept alive their spirit of vigil and prayer. As the medieval Latin *History of the Church of Durham* tells:

> The heathen overran the country on all sides and for many years dwelt within the land of Northumbria. Then the Christian men of that land, with their wives and children, followed in the pilgrimage of those who carried the body of St. Cuthbert, deeming that all the things which they had lost, country, homes, furnishings, were still theirs, if only they might keep with them this, their treasure.

4

These tidings, then, came to the king of Wessex from Northumbria. Other news was brought from across the border and from overseas, no less full of portent and fear. In Wales, Rhodri Mawr, Rhodri the Great, was steadily adding to his dominions. He had married Angharad, sister of the king of Ceredigion and Ystrad Tywi; and, when about 872 that king met his death by drowning, Rhodri saw in this a happy chance to annex his lands. In Ireland, through the work of Ivar the Boneless and the Norseman Olaf the White, of Norway's royal House of Vestfold, the pirate settlement at Dublin had ripened into a center, a kingdom, of Viking power, bursting with lust for further conquest. In Italy, the pope and the king-emperor, Louis the Second, had long been doing their utmost to defend its southern cities and monasteries from the Saracens. In France, Vikings had ceaselessly been busy for destruction in the region around the Loire, under a Danish chieftain named Haesten, who was to worry Alfred day and night in England long after this time.

The year 872 had brought these pirates on the Loire a special boon. As we saw before, the Scandinavian Vikings were not only roaming Europe in search of plunder. They were always seeking new colonies, new homes. Now, at Angers, on the river Maine, not far from its junction with the Loire, they had found a city empty and silent—for its citizens had fled from their approach—a stronghold fortified by water and by walls. Here, it had seemed to them, they might make for themselves a permanent dwelling, a Viking center in France, as their fellow-Scandinavians had done in Ireland, at Dublin and elsewhere, as they were doing in England, at York. Accordingly, they had brought their wives and children by boat along the Maine, had settled them there, had repaired and strengthened the ramparts of Angers, and with fresh zeal had turned to ravaging France from this, their city and their home.

Rumor of the new and sinister happening struck Charles the Bald, king of France, with fresh dismay. He could not bear the thought of Vikings at home in his city of Angers. In 873, when the Danes in England were plundering Mercia and its king was making ready to leave for Rome, Charles determined to drive out the evil, "growing as a malignant cancer in the very vitals of his realm." He asked aid from all his allies; he sent word "as to a kinsman in blood and in the Faith" to Salomon, ruler of Brittany, that he join him in this crusade. Salomon came. Many days passed as the two sat encamped on the bank of the Maine, facing a fortress apparently impregnable. Gloom deepened when a messenger arrived to inform Charles "in no uncertain words" that a multitude of locusts had appeared from the north darkening the skies of France, "a very plague of Egypt." Still the king held his ground. All possible devices of assault, catapults and battering rams, were brought into play upon the walls of Angers; but all were in vain. The ground was unfavorable; the Danes fought untiringly; plague broke out.

Then someone in the Frankish army hit upon a plan which at last turned despair and defeat into victory. Charles with renewed hope watched his engineers and sappers dig a channel, wide and deep, and divert into this the waters of the Maine. Soon the boats which all these weary days had brought provision to the Vikings within the walls of Angers were left high and dry. Promptly they surrendered. They gave money; they swore they would at once depart, never to return. This last promise they zealously broke. As the Frankish chronicle described it, "King Charles received their money, allowed their departure, and gave them the chance to do worse in time to come."

In 875, in compensation for his ever increasing anxieties, Charles won a prize which he had long been coveting. He outstripped his brother, Louis the German, in the race between them for land and honor and was crowned at Rome as emperor of the Franks by the pope, John the Eighth. It was Christmas Day. Doubtless Charles as he received the crown was thinking of another similar ceremony on Christmas Day, 800, and felt himself a second Charlemagne.

5

In England, those men of the great Danish host who did not march to occupy Northumbria with Halfdan— and they numbered very many—had left Repton in 874 for the fenlands of Cambridge, under three leaders, Guthrum, Oscytel, and Anund. They were still encamped there in the following summer when Alfred put out to sea, we are not told from where, fought a battle against seven Viking warships, captured one, and chased the rest in flight. An English force was meanwhile keeping watch in the fenlands; but the Danes slipped away secretly one dark autumn night in 875 and rode across country into Wessex. There they chose a site for their settling which was especially favorable, the town of Wareham in Dorsetshire. It commanded all the "Isle of Purbeck"; it was surrounded by great walls of earth and stone, still visible in part; it was protected on all sides, except the west, by the rivers Frome and Piddle.

Wessex was now again in crisis; the Danes were once more upon its soil. Alfred, however, felt it useless at this time to try to drive them out of Wareham. On their side, perhaps because as the months wore on they grew restless in this walled and rather remote place, they seemed entirely willing to agree to terms of peace, provided that the king paid them the money they demanded. This he reluctantly did. They then in their turn gave him the hostages he asked and swore a most solemn oath, upon the holy ring, the armlet which lay upon the altar of their gods, that they would leave his kingdom of Wessex. Since never before had they sworn by this sacred ring in making contract with any people outside their own, Alfred may well have taken new heart.

It was, once more, to no purpose. In all, they stayed a year at Wareham and then broke their word. December of 876 was approaching when they again gave the king's army the slip and fled away to fresh land of Wessex, in Devonshire. There they found another fortress, that of Exeter. Alfred pursued them with all speed but could not overtake them before they were behind Exeter's walls, safe for the winter months.

But, if safe, besieged and unsupported. Alfred's men were waiting for them outside those walls. And the Danish fleet, which had been moored near them for their aid, was no longer within reach. It had, indeed, started on its way to anchor in Devon waters but had been caught in a great storm off the wild and dangerous cliffs of

Swanage, on the Dorset coast near Poole Harbor. One hundred and twenty of its ships were wrecked.

Once again, therefore, and from the fortress of Exeter, the Danes made peace and swore to depart. This time they did leave Wessex. They rode into Mercia in August, 877, to stay in Gloucester, protected by the Cotswolds, the Forest of Dean, and the Severn, which here is flowing wide and deep toward the sea. The soil here is rich for farming; and soon they were driving the English of Mercia from their homesteads and making ready a new division of its land. Part of this was left under the rule of the submissive Ceolwulf; part was distributed for cultivation among individual Danes. Henceforward there were two Mercias. One, the western part, roughly measured, was still in a manner English, under an English ruler. It was not appropriated by the Danes, even though Ceolwulf was of their appointing. The other, the eastern part, was now Danish, occupied and possessed by Danish farmers.

It was now that the wave of Danish peril rose to its crest to break upon Alfred and his land of Wessex. The Danish army stayed at Gloucester until shortly after Twelfth Night, the sixth of January, 878, and then, as usual, stole away, going south to Chippenham on the river Avon in Wiltshire. Here, in one of the royal manors of Wessex, Alfred's sister had been married to Burhred, the Mercian king. Here Alfred frequently came to find delight in hunting through the forests around Chippenham and Melksham. Very probably he was here at this very moment of January, keeping Epiphanytide. Perhaps the Danes hoped to capture him and so to bring this war to a triumphant close.

The situation was critical in the extreme, not only for Wessex, but for all England. Eastern Mercia was lost. Northumbria was lost. There Halfdan, now sure of the land, had been doing what had been done in eastern Mercia, distributing acres for farming among his Danes. East Anglia, although not yet occupied in precise division, was a defeated kingdom. All now depended upon Wessex and its power to hold out and, what seemed impossible, its power to conquer the Danes, now intrenched on every side.

Not only in Wiltshire but in Wessex farther west the Danish enemy was in action. Early in this year of 878 another leader, described as another son of Ragnar Lothbrok and brother of Halfdan, sailed with twenty-three ships from Dyfed, the present Pembrokeshire in southwestern Wales, where he and his Danes had been spending the winter in raids, to begin similar descents upon the coast of Devon. If that fleet had not foundered off the Dorset coast and failed in support of its army on land, these raiders from South Wales might have swelled in hideous degree the force of their fellow-Danes in Exeter.

But the good news came to Alfred in this time of crisis that the invader had been defeated and killed. The men of Devon, it was said, commanded by their ealdorman, Odda, had fled from the enemy for refuge to a fortress now thought to have been standing on Countisbury Hill. Its ramparts were in bad repair, but its situation gave it protection on every side except the east. The Danes decided to take it by siege rather than by storm; those within, they thought, would yield very quickly, for there was no supply of water. It was mistaken reasoning. The men of Devon, inspired of God, Asser declares, chose battle with hope of victory rather than death by slow starvation. They rushed out one morning in the twilight of dawn, caught the enemy off guard, killed their leader, eight hundred of his fighting men, so report told, and forty of his retinue, and, as a final and magnificent triumph, captured from these Danes their Raven Banner.

Yet for those facing crisis in Wiltshire and in Somerset the possibility of defeat, final and decisive, was drawing ever nearer. From Wiltshire, from the Danish base at Chippenham, forays soon became so fierce and frequent that many dwellers in Wessex fled across the sea or, despairing even of that refuge, yielded themselves and their possessions to those invaders whom they now believed to hold in their grasp all the English land.

6

"Except Alfred the King," as the Anglo-Saxon chronicler proudly wrote. If Alfred was at Chippenham that January, he in some way outwitted his enemy. Some two months later, after Easter, which in 878 fell on the twenty-third of March, he and Ethelnoth, ealdorman of Somerset, led a small company of their most trusted and able men into the deep solitude of the Somerset marshes, to the "Isle of Athelney," near Taunton.

He who now makes pilgrimage to this place turns from the road on the bank of the river Tone, near its union with the Parret, crosses a farmyard, and in a moment finds himself on the moor marked by a stone memorial to the courage of this king of Wessex. On one side is the church of Lyng, for Athelney is in Lyng Parish; on the other stands the hill known as "The Mump," which bears on its summit the ruin of an eighteenth-century church, never completed, of St. Michael. All around, the land is covered with osiers and reeds. Here and there run water ducts in straight line, fringed by willows; on their banks are laid in rows the withies, drying for their weaving into baskets. At times the clouds brood low and dark over this lonely scene, and one feels even now a sense of danger and desolation rising from the past.

The land, of course, is now well drained, although it is still marshy, and winter and spring find it in places impassable because of pools of water. In Alfred's month of March, 878, all was swamp and flood. Here and there rose islands of higher ground, where now one finds villages, Chedzoy, Middlezoy, Stoke St. Gregory, Athelney itself. All in Alfred's time, except the necessary clearings, was one dense forest of alders.

Here the king made his camp for his time of need. The two rivers made a natural barrier for some measure of defense. Near the Parret he raised a fort, strongly built, and, we may think, threw across the river a rough bridge for the use of his men. Food was at hand in abundance. Not only were there deer and other game roaming everywhere through this forest, but on its clearings and islands were countless farms and pastures. Here worked loyal men of Wessex who brought wheat and milk and eggs, sheep and cattle, for the use of their king and who acted as guides to point out the various trails and tracks through the marsh. For this inner heart of Wessex had not suffered from Danish raids.

In its solitude and secrecy the king thought out his

purpose. Constantly his followers sallied out from this hidden stronghold to fall upon the Danes, who foraged here and there, to bring fear and uncertainty to them and to bring the harvest of wide scouting to Athelney. More needful still, as his thought grew gradually clearer in his mind, he sent out men, no doubt disguised as peasants, to tell his ealdormen, and bid them tell to others in their turn, the plans he had conceived, in their detail of place and day and hour, for that great and decisive battle for which they were to gather to meet him when the time was fully come.

From this time onward no one of the three leaders called sons of Ragnar Lothbrok, Ivar the Boneless, Half-dan, and the third, killed in 878, is encountered in our story. Neither are Oscytel and Anund, captain-kings in Cambridgeshire. Alfred, it would seem, as he pondered and planned in the marshes and alders of Athelney, was now facing the host of these Danish invaders under command of Guthrum alone.

As one might expect, legends arose around this retreat of this Saxon king at Athelney. One of these is known wherever Alfred's name is known: the story of King Alfred and the cakes. This told, in brief, that one day the king as he hunted for game in the forest came to the cottage of a peasant. The man was away at work, but Alfred asked of his wife, who did not recognize him, if he might rest a while by her hearth. He sat there, his hands busy in cleaning his bow and arrows, his thought, as ever, far away, while the woman went about her work in her home. Suddenly there rose a smell of burning. Alas! the buns which she had so carefully made and put to bake for her husband's supper were scorched black. She flew to rescue them, calling down malediction on the head of her unknown guest. "Quick enough, I warrant, you are to eat them, good and hot, you who do not move to keep my cakes from ruin by the fire!"

It is a story that ought to be true. Perhaps it is. But it is suspect as a tradition of post-Conquest days, told in the *Annals* of the monastery of that St. Neot who lived in Wessex during Alfred's ninth century. Unfortunately, the *Annals* and the "Lives" of St. Neot rest largely on fiction rather than on fact. Neot was said to have talked with Alfred, man to man on earth, and afterward, as he died shortly before the king retired to Athelney, to have appeared to him there in a vision to assure him of coming victory.

The north of England, also, told of a vision appearing to Alfred at Athelney; but this time the saint was the great Cuthbert, whom later ages especially connected with Alfred's reverence and devotion. It would not, indeed, be strange if the king during these days of waiting did think of those relics of Cuthbert, borne here and there through the north country to outwit and escape the Danes; if he did invoke the intercession of this saint, so widely revered, for the rescue of England; if perhaps Cuthbert did visit his dreams by night.

Finally, the tale of King Alfred entering from Athelney the Danish camp in disguise of a strolling player to bear away for his own future victory the enemy's secret plans is but a pleasant romance told by William of Malmesbury in his twelfth century.

7

Even in 878 for Alfred, as man and as king, there was hope. It had been far otherwise with Charles the Bald, whose perils from the Danes had constantly linked him with Alfred and whose tragic end in 877 now merits a word. At last his unceasing desire for new possessions, new dominions, had risen to destroy him. The death of his brother, Louis the German, in 876 had brought him, he hoped, fresh occasion for grasping. He had refused to meet his nephew, Louis the Younger, but had hurried with an army to Cologne, bent on his aim of seizing German land. There he had heard that this nephew was also on the bank of the Rhine, at Andernach. Charles had forced his own army to march by roads which were but mere trails, all through a night of pouring rain, to fall upon the camp of Louis at dawn. His men, weary and drenched to the skin, had been defeated. Naturally, tension of bitterness between Charles and his kinsmen of Germany had reached a new height.

There were other problems, equally hard to settle. From Italy had come a call that could not pass unheard. Pope John the Eighth had been sending continually to Charles his prayer, his demand, for aid against the Saracen invaders. "God crowned you by our hand, beloved son," the pope had written in May, 877, "for the defense of the Church against heathen assault. Now day by day we are suffering things beyond measure. All the Campagna is laid waste. Nothing is left for our sustenance, for ourselves, for monasteries and holy places, for the Senate of Rome." In France, Vikings on a hundred warships once more were at work along the Seine; in this same month of May, Charles had ordered for their appeasing exaction of tribute from state and church throughout his realm. There were personal hostilities, as well, lying heavy on the king's mind. He had offended his friend, Hincmar of Reims, by giving (in the pope's name) another archbishop precedence over Hincmar among the prelates of France. Hincmar had openly declared in council that this was against canon law, but his protest had availed him nothing. The nobles of France, spiritual and secular, were ever increasing in independence and ambition. Charles was forever trying to win them by gifts of lands, of castles, of abbeys for their rule, laymen though they were. Their power only grew the more, for his alarm and disquieting.

Amid all this distraction he decided to go to Italy for the cause of the pope. Hardly had he arrived there and had been welcomed by John the Eighth when terrifying news broke on his ears. Carloman, brother of that Louis whom he had lately attacked on the Rhine, had entered Italy at the head of an army. To Charles the only possible meaning of this was intent of retaliation, of war. He decided to return at once to France. His health had long been failing, and now, as he fled toward the Alpine passes, sudden sickness came upon him. For eleven days he lay in a wretched hut, the only shelter he could reach. On the sixth of October he died in agony. Men said that his favorite physician, a Jew named Zedekiah, had given him a draught of poison.

His body was at once embalmed as best might be contrived, thrust into a coffin, and borne forward on the journey to Paris for burial at Saint-Denis. Soon the bearers were forced to stop—*pro foetore non valentes portare*—as Hincmar wrote. It was then inclosed in a stout cask, thickly coated inside and out with pitch. *Quod nihil ad tollendum foetorem profecit.* Suddenly the men put their burden down. They would carry it no longer; and Charles, king of France, emperor of the Franks, scholar of theology, of Latin culture and learning, was hastily buried by kindness of a few monks in Burgundy.

8

Seven weeks went by at Athelney; but even in so short a time Alfred was ready. In May of 878, during Ascensiontide, he and his followers rode out from the marshes to "Egbert's Stone," probably near Penselwood, Somerset, on the border of Wiltshire. Nowadays the traveler seeking the same goal journeys from Athelney in the direction of Somerton, Keinton Mandeville, and Castle Cary. Near Penselwood, which rests on high ground, runs the river Stour, and in Stourhead Park, hard by the village of Stourton in Wiltshire, there now stands the eighteenth-century "King Alfred's Tower." At "Egbert's Stone," as Alfred had planned, gathered on this day all men of Somerset and of Wiltshire who could bear arms and many from Hampshire. There they met the king, and, as Anglo-Saxon record simply and vividly put it, "they were fain of him"—*his gefægene wæron*—"they were glad to see him." Asser, who had the story from Alfred, said that they welcomed him as one risen from the dead. One night he stayed there and on the morrow marched on to "Iglea," afterward known as Iley Oak, probably where Southleigh Wood, or Eastleigh Wood, now lies, near Bishopstrow in Wiltshire. At dawn of the next day the king's army was again moving. Finally it came to a halt at Edington, also in Wiltshire, close to Westbury.

Here, from above, the ancient camp of Bratton Castle and another White Horse, cut on the slope, still look down. This Horse, as it now appears, dates from the eighteenth century; but, as at Uffington, some figure of a horse may have been here as far back as the time of the Belgae. In any case, the White Horse of Westbury was not first cut for the praise of Alfred, greatly as he was to deserve that praise.

At Edington, Alfred met the Danes under Guthrum and, as Asser tells us, "closed his ranks, shield locked with shield, and fought fiercely against the entire heathen host in long and stubborn stand. At last by God's will he won his victory, slew very many, and pursued the rest to their place of refuge, striking as he went. All things which he came upon outside this shelter, men and horses and cattle, he made his own. The men he killed, the beasts he captured, and then pitched camp boldly with all his army before the gates of the fortress held by the heathen."

This fortress was Chippenham, the Danish base, some fifteen miles from Edington. For fourteen days Alfred and his men blockaded the Danes encamped within its walls, until, starving, cold, and hopeless of relief, they surrendered and yielded hostages in surety of their word. That they swore to depart from Wessex was an old story; but new was the promise of Guthrum, their king, to yield allegiance to the Christian church. Both promises were kept. Three weeks later Guthrum went with twenty-nine chosen men of his army to Aller, now a village lying below High Ham Hill, near Athelney, and there was baptized and anointed with holy oil. The white linen band of chrism was bound around his forehead, and King Alfred received him from the font as his son in the faith, with a new Anglo-Saxon, Christian name of Athelstan. For seven days Guthrum wore the white of the newly baptized, and on the eighth, at Wedmore, near Cheddar and the river Axe, the "chrism-loosing," the unbinding of the fillet, was celebrated in the presence of Ealdorman Ethelnoth as spiritual friend and host. High feasting followed, and the Danish leader stayed in Wedmore twelve days with Alfred, his conqueror and godfather, who honored him as king and warrior with gifts, many and rich.

9

It was a great victory. Alfred well might feast and be joyful. The weeks of his thinking and planning in the solitude of the Athelney marshes had done their work, and peace was in sight. Now he could make treaty with Guthrum and his Danes for their departure, as he hoped, without return.

His hope was in part fulfilled. The storm which had raged so long did not die down in permanence or at once. Guthrum made covenant to lead his army out of Wessex and to ravage its land no more. But he led it only as far as western Mercia, where it settled at Cirencester, in Gloucestershire, and stayed there a year. This was under the rule of the English Ceolwulf, and therefore the invaders, conquered as they were, were still upon ground nominally English. They left at last in the autumn of 879 for East Anglia, which they now made entirely theirs by permanent occupation, dividing it out among those of their men who wanted to stay and make this foreign land their home.

While Guthrum's army had been in Gloucestershire, another fleet of Danish ships had come sailing from the Continent to anchor in the Thames. Their men encamped for the winter of 878–79 at Fulham, on the river. It is interesting to read that the force at Fulham in the east of England actually met in conference with Guthrum. But it did not join him in the west; it remained at Fulham. It even departed again across the Channel just about the time when Guthrum went with his men into East Anglia. Probably we may see the influence of Guthrum here. He had, it would seem, at the moment no thought of a union of Danish forces in renewal of the struggle. It would be better, he evidently decided, for a while to strengthen the Danish hold upon East Anglia by settling Danish farmers there, as they had been settled in eastern Mercia and in Northumbria.

The next years saw increasing hope for Wessex but continuing misery for the Continent in their common wrestling with invasion. From Rome the pope, John the Eighth, wrote in 882 to Richilde, widow of Charles the Bald, of his despair at the Saracen approach: "We have looked for light, and behold, darkness; we have sought help, and we dare not leave the walls of our City. Over us rages a storm of assault intolerable, beyond endurance. Neither our spiritual son, the Emperor, nor any other man of any nation appears for our aid. We see advancing upon us an army, not twofold, but even threefold, fourfold. Unless high Heaven comes to our rescue, we shall be compelled to ask of the enemy their terms of peace. If not, of a certainty we shall be driven captive beneath their yoke, and then they will not scruple to cut our throats." In December of that year the pope was dead. The *Annals* of Fulda, whether truly or not, declared that he was murdered: that one of his relatives, eager to seize his wealth and even his office, gave him a drink of poison and, when this did not promptly bring death, finished the work by striking him with a hammer on the head.

In the same year, 882, the march of the Scandinavian Vikings toward Reims drove Hincmar, its archbishop, from his see. As he fled, he carried with him the bones of St. Remigius, patron of Reims, across the Marne and through the forest to Epernay, where just before Christmas he, too, died. His successor, Fulk, was, like him, to play a leading part among the nobles of France.

Three years later the Danes were once more at the gates of Paris, determined on its capture by siege, however long, however costly. It was their hour of fortune. The crown of France, and of all the empire of the west, was resting on the incapable head of another nephew of Charles the Bald known as Charles the Fat. There had been by this time no other for France to elect. To him Fulk now appealed: "Unless God in his mercy helps us," he wrote, "Paris will soon be taken and all our kingdom will be lost."

But for nearly a year, from November, 885, until late in 886, Charles the Fat, king of France and emperor, delayed his coming, while the Danes fought furiously against his city. With heroic courage the men of France fought back, led by Eudes, count of Paris, and Joscelin, its bishop. Fortifications rose in ceaseless working, day and night, for the defense of either side; missiles flew hour by hour; fire and flood burst upon the besieged; famine made resistance almost impossible. In April the bishop could endure no more, and died. Eudes sent a last message to Charles: "The city is on the point of falling." In October the king arrived. Then "a matter truly miserable was brought to pass. Seven hundred pounds were paid in silver to the invaders for the release of Paris from siege, and the way was opened to them without let or hindrance to spend a winter of ravaging in Burgundy."

His capitulation to the Danes cost Charles his throne. His nobles, disgusted at his lack of courage and decision, in 887 agreed that they would have no more of him. They drove him out, and, after much strife of parties, Eudes, the brave defender of Paris, was crowned to rule France at Compiègne in February, 888.

By that time Charles, too, had died. His departure from the scene brought to an end the union of Frankish realms under the Carolingian House. As Regino, abbot of Prüm in the diocese of Trier, shrewdly wrote: "Since he is dead the kingdoms under his rule, as if bereft of lawful inheritor, are no longer one compacted body, but are broken into pieces. No longer do they look forward to one Lord, ordained by nature; rather, each single realm is busy to create from within itself its own individual king."

10

In England, slowly but surely, the dawn of a day of peace was rising. In 882 Alfred fought a naval battle against four Danish ships. Two of them he captured, and killed all they carried. The leaders and men on the other two fought until wounds and exhaustion forced them to surrender.

Two years afterward Danes again crossed the Channel to lay siege to Rochester, in Kent, open to approach both by the river Medway and by the old Roman road between London and the Kentish coast. The men of Rochester held out all through the winter of 884–85, the more courageous a stand in that, as so often, the Viking besiegers had built strong ramparts for their own defense around their camp outside its walls. Nevertheless, they fled when Alfred arrived, in the spring, with a great army for the city's relief. So quickly did they hasten to their ships, moored on the river nearby, that all their horses, which they had brought with them from the Continent, and many prisoners, too, they left behind them, to be welcomed by Alfred and his captains. Once on board, they made with all speed for France.

This assault upon Rochester was apparently too strong a temptation for Guthrum to resist. Doubtless he was weary of that dull work of settling East Anglia. Some of the Danes, also, who had been besieging Rochester had not fled overseas; they were still lurking here and there in the woods along the south bank of the Thames, attacking farms and villages in raids. Now "the Danish host in East Anglia broke peace with Alfred the King," and for his country's defense Alfred sent every seaworthy craft he could muster to attack and capture the Danish fleet off that coast. At the mouth of the river Stour his men met sixteen warships of the enemy, fought them with relentless vigor, and took them all as prize, with everything on and in them. Success, however, seems to have relaxed English vigilance. Now Guthrum, thwarted and angry, gathered on his part every Viking boat within reach for his revenge. As Alfred's fleet, heavily laden, was slowly plowing its way home, it fell in with these Vikings, panting for battle, and lost all it had won.

But this was not the end. Defeat, after his victories in Wessex, drove Alfred to use all his force in one sweeping and determined action. Quickly he marched "with burning of towns and killing of men" upon London itself. Nor did he rest until in the next year, 886, it was in his hands, half-ruined, unfit for decent dwelling, but his. For the work of restoration and for its future ruling the king gave it into the charge of his devoted friend, Ethelred, ealdorman of English Mercia.

Here was a definite assurance of victory, and its consequences were great. Now "all the English people submitted to Alfred, except those who were under holding of Danish men." Now Guthrum sought a new treaty of peace, and this was made, in different and far more definite terms than had been accepted after the battles at Edington and Chippenham. The terms we will consider in connection with Alfred's laws for his country. At the moment the important point to note is that henceforth England, for occupation and for rule, was divided into two parts, English and Danish, and that Alfred left the

Danish rulers of his time free to govern their own people as they would, provided that they remained within the bounds laid down and kept the terms of the treaty now established. The line between the two parts ran, according to this agreement, "along the river Thames, then along the river Lea to its source, then direct to Bedford, then along the Ouse to Watling Street."

To the lands included in this agreement for occupation under Guthrum must be added territory, such as that in the north, already held by the Danes. Henceforth, then, the Danes held Essex, East Anglia, the Eastern Midlands (with Lincolnshire), and the land north of the Humber. Alfred was king in the south, from Cornwall to the regions in the east, south of the Thames; and, with delegated authority, over the western Midlands, the English Mercia ruled for him by Ethelred, extending east to Watling Street, north to the Mersey, west to the Welsh border, south into Gloucestershire. Ceolwulf, "the foolish thane," now disappears from history.

This is a rough description, and there are exceptions within its bounds. But it gives in outline the land over which Alfred now held his charge. Much had been lost, but much had been saved. Alfred was king over his England, and there was peace. The time had now come when he could turn from the defending of his people and country, from the fear of their capture and destruction, to the thought and care of their domestic life and well-being, of their government, their education, their political, social, and spiritual health.

CHAPTER FIVE

King Alfred AND HIS RULE IN WESSEX

IN THIS ANGLO-SAXON Wessex under Alfred, as in Anglo-Saxon England in general, society was both divided and linked together by rank, ecclesiastical and secular. At the head of all its people stood the king; and below him stood bishops, ealdormen, lesser nobles, priests and ministers, the ceorls, or freemen who worked for their living in trade or on the land, and, finally, the serfs, or slaves. Every free man and woman, from the king downward, was assessed at his wergild, his "man-price," the amount at which his value to society in terms of money was registered by his government for the purpose of its laws; in practice, the amount prescribed by law as payable in compensation for hurt done to him and for hurt done by him.

In this ranking we see the ordered dividing of Anglo-Saxon society. Its union is seen, as it was seen in that older Germanic custom on the Continent of which the Saxons of England still bore the mark, in the aid and protection given by those of higher rank to those under them, those who were attached to their service and owed them loyalty. The king stood for the protection of all and, especially, of those nearest to him, the bishops who governed his dioceses, the ealdormen who governed his shires, the nobles who held office in his court and household. Under the king his secular nobles and ministers held responsibility for those under them. Bishops answered for their clergy; abbots for their monks; landowners for the ceorls who labored on their estates.

When, therefore, a man stood accused before a court of law, he looked to him who was over and above him, that is, to his lord: first, to swear to his innocence, if he wished to defend himself against the charge declared in court; second, if he admitted his guilt, to make whole or part payment of the compensation or fine by which his offense was punished. Should this crime have cost the life of another, the amount exacted in reparation corresponded to the dead man's wergild, his value in money to his world. This reparation was made to the relatives of the dead. Similar compensation, in a lesser amount, was required in cases of wilful injury short of death.

There was a second source of protection and aid for the Anglo-Saxon when hurt or accused of wrongdoing. This stood in blood relationship, that bond of kindred between members of the family or clan, which was, also, closely knit among all Germanic peoples. The bond of a man with his kinsfolk was even stronger than that between a man and his lord; to his lord the man who had no kinsfolk at his call looked for support. The relatives of a man injured or killed exacted by right of law, and received, wergild from his assailant. On the other hand, they swore in the court of law their oaths to clear their kinsman from charge and, if he were judged guilty, contributed to the payment of wergild in compensation for his crime.

Sometimes, however, kinsfolk took the punishing of crime wrought against one of their blood into their own hands. The blood feud, fiercely pursued in early Anglo-Saxon days, still existed in Alfred's time. It was not so freely carried on as formerly, however, because the restraining hand of Alfred's laws did its best to protect those in danger from angry relatives.

Church and state worked together in the administration of law. Ealdormen and bishops not only fought side by side in war to defend their country, but sat side by side to try secular offenders in its courts, to ponder matters of government in its councils. The most solemn offices of the church were called upon in the endeavor to decide at the altar itself the question of a man's innocence or guilt; and a criminal was safe, at least for the time, if he could reach sanctuary within holy walls. For the church, though she shared the sternness of the law, worked also to temper its rigor with mercy. She recognized the Christian rights of serfs, those laborers bound to their owners and to the soil on which they lived. Poverty, inability to pay compensation of wergild for crime committed, capture in war, had brought them to this durance of bondage; but the church knew them as baptized members of her fold, required of them obedience to her precepts and rules, and admitted them to her sacramental life.

The king was represented in judgment of law by an ealdorman in each shire. To share in this judgment and to unite with the crown in giving forth law on matters spiritual for the people, Alfred, like his father, Ethelwulf, had two bishops for Wessex proper, one seated at Winchester in Hampshire, the other at Sherborne in Dorset. Above these in dignity and in association with the king was the archbishop of Canterbury, also of Alfred's sphere of jurisdiction in his later days; and working in fellowship with Wessex under Alfred were the bishops of London, Rochester, and Mercian Dorchester. The chief lords and ministers of Wessex, spiritual and temporal, made up its council, its witan, the assembly of counselors on whom the king called for advice in matters of importance.

Such, in outline, was the basis of the organizing of Wessex under Alfred. It was his duty and concern on this basis to build a government which should meet the problems of his time. And these problems were many. Now, in 886, his kingdom had been under invasion for more than fifty years. Its men had been killed, its buildings destroyed, its fields scoured and spoiled, year after year. The heart of Wessex, it is true, had escaped, guarded by forest, lake, and marsh; but its towns, Southampton and Exeter, Rochester, Reading, London, had known the force of the enemy. The countryside of Wiltshire, of Berkshire, of Dorsetshire, of Hampshire, of Kent, had been occupied or raided or fought over as long as men could recall. Ruins were crying for restoration in unnumbered places. Nor was this the worst. The many years of war had changed men's habits and customs, had slackened their zeal for industry in the old ways of peace, had quickened their minds and their hands for fighting, had lessened their self-control. The transition from military life under actual war to a life of peace which must always be ready for fresh outbreak of war was difficult for a land which was defended by a fyrd, a national army made up from its nobles and farmers, its laborers and peasants at large.

2

So Alfred gave all his endeavor to the compiling of laws for his disorganized people. His code, which we still have in its Anglo-Saxon words, was made toward the end of his reign, perhaps about 890, although the exact date is not known. In an introduction he declared that his laws were based upon the Ten Commandments given by God to Moses; fulfilled and interpreted by the love and compassion of his Son, the Healer, the Lord Christ; continued in the teachings of the Apostles, and thence down the ages by synods of the church and decrees of kings. He had drawn, he added, upon the best which he had found in the laws of Ine, "my kinsman" (king of Wessex from 688 to 726), of Offa, king of Mercia, and of Ethelbert, "who first among its kings received baptism in England." Finally, all his counselors had approved this code of his and had given consent for its observance throughout Wessex.

The king began his code by emphasizing the sanctity and solemnity of a man's oath: "Most necessary is it that every man keep with due care his oath and his pledge." Should he break his word, once given before due witness, his bishop might punish him in prison for forty days, where he would be entirely dependent for food upon his own resources or, if he had none, upon the good will of his relatives. Should he be accused of breaking a contract witnessed and blessed by the church, his accuser must declare the charge aloud in four churches; and the accused, if he would maintain his innocence, must declare this on oath in twelve churches. Whichever of the two parties was eventually held to be lying incurred punishment not only for his original offense but also for perjury and desecration of God's holy place.

Only in the case of a pledge wickedly made against the law, especially one involving treason, that is, plotting against his lord, could a man rightly renounce his plighted word. For treason was worse than murder in the code of the Anglo-Saxon Alfred. Above all, the king's person was sacred. Death was the penalty, deliberately laid down by Alfred, for one who either himself purposed in mind and act death for his king or gave shelter to any man, outlaw or retainer or citizen of any kind, guilty of such crime. Only the complete clearing of the accused from this charge before his judges could save his life; and this clearing could only be brought about through the attesting of his innocence by oath of witness able to pledge in support of his, or their, oath a sum of money equal to the royal wergild, the very heavy "man-value" set upon the life of the king. Death could also be inflicted at the king's pleasure upon anyone who fought or even drew sword in the royal hall.

Next to the iniquity of treason against the king was the guilt of the man who plotted against his lord, of whatever rank. For him both life and all he owned were lawfully forfeit, unless he, also, could clear himself by oath, offering pledge of his lord's wergild in its support.

Murder, when not aggravated by treason, brought upon the offender necessity of heavy compensation to the family of the victim. Alfred was eager to allow such penalty of fine instead of death even for this capital crime. If the victim had met his fate amid a band of robbers, his "man-price," as well as a fine, was due from the robber who actually struck the blow; but a fine was imposed also on every one of his companions for the sin of belonging to such a band. A man who killed another in a fight and had no relatives on his father's side must hope to gain aid from his mother's kin for payment of wergild in reparation to the dead man's family. If a murder was committed with a weapon borrowed from a friend, the lender fell under penalty together with the murderer, unless he could present witness of oath to the satisfaction of the court that he had been entirely ignorant of the purpose of the loan. He who killed a pregnant woman paid her own full "man-value" and half its father's value for the child she was carrying in her womb. A priest who committed murder was unfrocked, unless his lord was willing to offer reparation for him of his victim's price.

There is a very long list in these laws of Alfred of punishments, by fine, for injuries done in violence to every part of a man's body. One reads here of the payments inflicted for thrashing an innocent man of the common people; for cutting his hair to make him look unsightly; for tonsuring him in mockery; for cutting off his beard; for striking off his ear or nose or one of his fingers. The injury to a finger was punished according to a scale of values. Loss of a third finger brought the heaviest fine, since it bore a man's ring; then, in descending order of importance, came the first, the middle, the little finger. But the thumb, of course, cost by far the most to the sinner. In the same manner, he who in a passion of anger knocked out his neighbor's tooth paid compensation according to its position, less for one in the back, more for one in the front; loss of an eyetooth brought especially heavy penalty. Other fines met those who knocked out an eye, or blinded a man in the eye without knocking it out; who deliberately broke another's jaw bone or chin bone; who tore out a tongue, or pierced a throat, or ripped off a finger nail.

Accidental injury also found its place in Alfred's code and was treated here in a way which reminds us of the law of Deuteronomy. There were complicated regulations governing wounds inflicted by a man carrying a spear on his shoulder, according to the verdict of deliberate or unintentional harming. If a tree fell and killed a man who was working with another, the kindred of the dead received the tree as compensation, provided that they carried it away within thirty days. Owners of vicious dogs kept them at their own risk. If such a dog attacked anyone with serious result, its owner paid a heavy fine, and a fine increasingly heavier for each successive onset. Apparently he might continue to keep his dog. If, however, the dog disappeared after doing the damage, the fine had to be paid just the same. We are not told what happened when a neighbor openly killed the dog. The owner of a bull or an angry cow which injured anyone was ordered to hand over the animal to the wounded man, unless money was paid in an acceptable sum.

Fighting was strictly limited. Fines were imposed on those who disturbed the peace of a public meeting at which someone of importance was present. The insult was expiated in accordance with the rank of the person thus insulted. To fight in the presence of an archbishop cost a large sum; then came bishop or ealdorman, ranked equally, then lesser magistrate or priest in the royal service. A fight in the house of a simple citizen required a comparatively small payment to the innocent goodman of the house. Fines, likewise, were the fate of anyone who dared to injure a person under the protection of archbishop or bishop or ealdorman.

Injuries to a woman, short of death, were restricted here to sexual crime. The wife-beater, it would seem, incurred no sentence in law; but both men and women were punished for sin against morality. The man who seduced another's wife paid compensation to her husband according to the husband's rank. The wife was presumed innocent. A young woman, however, who after her solemn pledging to marriage was guilty of illicit relations outside her bond paid for her sin in livestock according to her own money value to society. So, also, a man, if he insulted or raped her, paid to her a compensation of higher or lower amount, in keeping with her rank and the enormity of his offense. To do violence to a nun, of course, cost double; and whoever took a nun from her convent "without leave from the king or the bishop" paid heavily to king, to bishop, and to the head of the convent. Neither the nun in question nor any child she might bear could inherit any property belonging to her abductor. Fine, also, was paid by one who raped a slave girl, and compensation was made as well to her owner. If her seducer was himself a slave, he was punished by castration. Slaves were punished without redress; their secular rights, indeed, were almost entirely the privilege of those who possessed and sold them as chattels of exchange.

Theft was one of the most common offenses against Alfred's laws. An interesting clause declares: "Formerly to steal gold or horses or bees brought higher fines. Now all thefts, except the abducting of human beings, meet the same penalty." He to whom a sword or a tool was intrusted for its polishing, sharpening, or repair was responsible for its good condition upon return. Traders were responsible for the honesty of the assistants who traveled with them to serve their business; heirs were bound to abide by the conditions of bequest; he who wished to transfer his service from one place and one lord to another place and lord must first obtain leave from the ealdorman of his shire.

As we have seen, Alfred did all he could to replace summary justice, the "justice" of the blood feud, by justice administered in a court of law. He did not, indeed, altogether forbid his people to seek their own vengeance; he tried, rather, to control this so far as possible. A man might march to the home of one who had clearly wronged him and hold him prisoner there for as long as a month, provided that the prisoner's friends were given the chance to induce him, and aid him, to make due reparation for his wrongdoing. If he refused to do so, the man he had wronged might resort to violence without objection of the law. To fight for one's lord was also lawful, or for one's kindred, in case of need; as, for example, against the seducer of one's wife or daughter or mother; yet such fighting could not lawfully be followed by a blood feud between families. Crimes committed by the dumb or deaf who could not speak to declare their innocence or confess their guilt were, if possible, expiated by their fathers.

The church received its due reverence from these decrees of Alfred. Men were ordered holiday from all but necessary work for twelve days at Yuletide, from Christmas Day until Twelfth Night was past; on the fifteenth of February, marked in Anglo-Saxon calendars as "the day when Christ overcame the Devil"; on the twelfth of March, Feast of St. Gregory the Great, who had brought about the conversion of the English; during Holy Week and Easter Week; on the twenty-ninth of June, Feast of St. Peter and St. Paul; in the autumn, the full week before the Feast of Mary, Mother of the Lord, probably of her Assumption, on the fifteenth of August, rather than of her Nativity, on the eighth of September; on All Saints' Day, November the first. Slaves were not free on these days, but they were granted remission from work on the Wednesdays of the four Ember seasons of the year for the selling of articles given them or made by them in their scanty moments of leisure. Lent was ordered by both church and state as a time of strict praying and strict living. To break deliberately the church's laws during Lent brought a heavy fine upon the offender; and he who committed theft or burglary "during the army's absence from home on service," or during Lent, Christmas, Easter, Rogationtide, or Ascension Day or on any Sunday, was fined a double amount. The man who stole from a church was sentenced to lose the hand which did the deed, unless the court in mercy allowed him to redeem it by money.

Alfred also brought the power of his state to the support of the church in its long fight against magic and witchcraft. In obedience to the command in Exodus, "Do not let magicians live," he ordered in the Introduction to these laws that women who aided and favored practitioners and purveyors of spells and sorceries should be put to death.

We possess the text of a pact drawn up between Alfred and Guthrum the Dane which settled the boundaries of their respective territories and dealt with other matters. This represents, it would seem, the agreement made after London had been recaptured by Alfred in 886. In it the inhabitants of the kingdom of Guthrum, all Englishmen and Danes subject to his rule, were divided into two classes, one of higher, the other of lower, rank and standing. To each class a wergild corresponding to its higher or lower rank was assigned. The lives of all, therefore, whether Englishman or Dane, within each class were assessed at the same value. No man, whether free or slave, was allowed to pass between the two kingdoms, in either direction, without special leave, except for purposes of trade; and even in this case a pledge of honest and law-abiding intention was exacted before admission could be granted.

3

From compiling a code for his people the king turned with all his energy to this code's zealous and informed administration under the hands of his officials and representatives. Over the ealdormen and bishops who, without the co-operation of a "jury" in the modern sense, presided at the deciding of lawsuits and criminal charges in the "folk-moot," the public meeting of the people of a town or district; over the great landowners who heard accusations of minor importance proffered in their domains; over the king's reeves who had charge of the royal estates, who presided at the "folk-moot" for the settling of questions of trade and business—over all these Alfred kept strict and constant watch. Many were the disputes referred to him for arbitration, and often with dismay on one side or the other, for he was known as a just but unrelenting judge. In a letter addressed after Alfred's death to his son and successor, Edward the Elder, the writer referred to Edward's attention a claim brought before Alfred when he "was washing his hands in his room" at the manor of Wardour in Wiltshire. This claim was now being disputed. "Sire," asks the writer, "if one wants to change every judgment which King Alfred decreed, when will any claim be decided?"

Many were the officials whom this king called to his presence to hear their defense against charges of stupidity, indifference, or even outright dishonesty. From these he discovered by patient questioning the cause of the trouble, whether fear, or greed, or prejudice, or sheer ignorance. Among all these sins it was that of ignorance which drove Alfred nearer than any other to the losing of his kingly temper. Frequently he threatened dismissal to a magistrate or steward in his service who would not take the trouble to learn the rules of his job. Next to ignorance he detested laziness, sloth, idleness of any sort; and he used every means in his power to awaken all around him to that sense of the needful and the urgent which burned continually in his own heart. Fair words and sharp, persuasion and command, followed one another as he strove to convince his dull and unresponsive, his stubborn and unscrupulous courtiers. Occasionally he reached a point when he could bear no more. Then he burst out into a denunciation of folly and blindness which terrified all within reach of his scathing tongue.

No one, however, could be more considerate toward those in service under him. He divided into three companies all those, secular and spiritual, who held office in his household, in his royal chapel, in his court, and ordered that those in each division should be on duty, day and night, for a month, and should then return to their homes and estates, free from service for the two months to come. The same principle was applied for the inducing of greater efficiency and staying power in the national army of Wessex, made up of nobles and farmers and laborers on the land. These the king also separated into two great divisions with alternating duty. Henceforth half of his fighting men in days of war were away at the front; the other half remained at home, to care, in their different ways, as owner or as peasant, for the harvests, the herds and the flocks. Thus those who fought did so the more readily, both in the relief of rotating change and in the knowledge that the earth and its creatures which supported them and their families were not suffering by neglect. A spirit of enthusiasm for service in time of war was also present at court in the young men, sons of nobles, who were attached to the person of the king and lived in his household for their training in arms and for attendance on the throne. Such had been the custom in Germanic lands on the Continent from the time of the Roman Empire.

Defense from invading enemies was in Alfred's view the duty and concern of all men of Wessex, whether by fighting in the field or by guarding the land and its towns and villages. With this in mind he planned a building of fortresses throughout his realm. These were held and manned by fighters from the districts in which they stood, each fortress receiving a garrison in proportion to the length of its walls. The men who thus did service at home were exempt from the ordinary call to battle of the national army. Alfred did not live to complete this purpose; it was left to his son, Edward the Elder, to bring it into full working throughout Wessex. Even while he lived, moreover, the king encountered much difficulty in carrying it forward. We are told by Asser that co-operation in this part of his work for defense was lacking among his people; that fortresses he had ordered to be built were left unfinished, even unbegun, and this, too, in time of leisure and quiet.

4

It was now time for this king to consider in Wessex the problems of its days of peace: of new houses, new churches, new monasteries, in a land unsightly through ruins and crumbling walls. Asser is now again our author-ity. London and other cities were rebuilt; towns were planned and constructed. Enthusiasm, as was natural, rose high for this work among the many who longed for new and better homes. And at times, when he saw cause, the king allowed himself visions of beauty, of comeliness in strength. We read of his designs in gold and silver metal, for the adorning, no doubt, of palaces and cathe-drals, of his royal halls and chambers decorated with work in stone, timbered and paneled in wood. He even ordered certain of his royal manor houses to be moved from their sites into more beautiful surroundings, to be raised once more in different, even splendid style. A king, he believed, for his own and his people's sake, should be fittingly seated and throned.

Of the churches built and rebuilt by Alfred, none re-mains. But, fortunately, we have a description of one which he ordered made "in a new fashion" for a monas-tery founded by him at Athelney, in fulfilment, it was said, of a vow of thanksgiving for his victory. Its center was a circular space, outside which stood four posts, planted deep in the earth for the support of four rounded arches which rose from these posts or pillars on the four sides of the building.

This church is of special interest in that it shows dis-tinctly the influence of France in Carolingian days, of a France herself indebted in matters of art to Constantino-ple and the East. Here we see one instance among many of that extraordinary use by King Alfred of all sources of culture at his command, in Britain, in Ireland, on the Continent, in the East; of his constant keeping in touch with men and their movements in lands across the sea. We know from Asser that he brought artists and craftsmen from abroad to work in his kingdom and that he paid them from his own purse. His eager, restless mind thus drew from without whatever could be drawn, wherever this might be found. He used this in the service of his country, he gave it his country's stamp, he absorbed it, and he made it part of English heritage for the time to come.

This vision and care are seen, then, not only in building but in art and craftsmanship, the delight and constant study of this king. To each of the bishops of his realm he sent, with a book, the gift of a gold *æstel*, either, as has been suggested, as a marker to note the reader's place, or as a pointer to trace his progress, or as a weight to hold down his page. In the Ashmolean Museum at Oxford there are now two "jewels" connected with Alfred's time. One is known as the "Alfred Jewel," found in 1693 in the parish of North Newton near Athelney, Somerset, and subject ever since to discussion among scholars. Around it in letters of openwork design run the words:

ÆLFRED MEC HEHT GEWYRCAN,

"Alfred ordered me to be made." The whole is wrought in gold and cloisonné enamel, a little over two inches in length. On one side against a blue background there is a figure, dressed in green and reddish-brown, bearing in either hand a staff or scepter. Various suggestions have held this to be Alfred himself, or the Lord Christ, or one of his saints. The last theory seems perhaps the most likely. The other side is covered with gold, adorned with a delicate branching pattern. The base is shaped into a boar's head and ends in a socket, designed to receive a stem. To what use this "jewel" was put has never been decided. Perhaps it was attached to some altar, or statue, or vestment in the church at Athelney; perhaps Alfred himself carried it on his helmet or his crown. In it, once more, is seen the influence of Continental work, of France and of Italy. The other "jewel" was found at Minster Lovell in Oxfordshire about the mid-nineteenth century. It bears a cross, also in cloisonné enamel, and its sides show ornament of filigree in gold.

Also of great interest for the history of art in Alfred's reign is the evolving character of its work on stone. Here we may trace a progress from the baroque, lavishly decorated, animal patterns of the Saxon carvings in relief at Colerne in Wiltshire, from the richness of King Ethelwulf's gifts to Rome, from the elaborate designs of the rings of Ethelwulf and his daughter in the British Museum, to the newer manner heralded in the interlacing vines which twine around the animals on the fragments of the cross-shaft at Ramsbury, Wiltshire. Here is the beginning. It was slowly to move forward toward its fulfilling: toward the quiet and severe yet appealing beauty and dignity of the winged angel of Deerhurst in Gloucestershire, dated shortly after the turn of the ninth century to the tenth; toward the quick energy and lovely realism of the figures on the stole embroidered before 916 by order of Aelfflaed, wife of Edward the Elder, for Frithestan, bishop of Winchester, and now in the Cathedral Library at Durham; and, finally, toward the flowering, later in this tenth century, of Anglo-Saxon art into new vigor of Benedictine life.

In this progress we may see Alfred playing an indirect but impelling part. It was his love of English life and English character, as he knew it, which caused his sculptors, Englishmen trained under inspiration of France and Italy, to put into their art that quick and natural delight seen in the "dancing man" who carries so gaily his leafy branch at Codford St. Peter, Wiltshire. It was his hatred of the "overmuch" and the artificial which deterred Englishmen from overgreat enjoyment of the extravagances of Scandinavian carving, then at work in Ireland. It was his passion for the basic ideal of the art of Rome which taught him, and through him impressed upon the art of Wessex in his time, the lessons of simplicity, of economy, of the beauty of life in action, tense and exuberant, yet held always under restraint.

CHAPTER SIX

King Alfred AND HIS SCHOLARS AND TEACHERS

ALL HIS LIFE Alfred bitterly lamented the fact that he had not been properly taught in his childhood and youth. In the midst of the manifold duties which met him on every side, he insisted as king on saving time daily for making up, so far as he could, what he had so sorely missed and longed to possess. As a little boy we have found him learning by heart Anglo-Saxon poetry, and this he continued ever afterward and urged upon his friends, upon the ministers and officials of his court. Those among them who knew something of books he eagerly sought, bishops and secular nobles, for the enlightenment they could give him. The sons of some of these nobles lived as members of the royal household in order that they might begin early to read and to value the Latin manuscripts which at their age, and even still, their king understood but dimly and through the aid of learned men.

His own insufficiency, a vexation to him in his younger years, weighed far more heavily on his mind after he became ruler of Wessex. It was hard to face a country marred by physical ruin; it was far harder to rule a people steeped in ignorance, unaware of books. And this ignorance had not been true of the past. In the seventh and the eighth centuries the learning of England had stood high. That was a Golden Age, when Theodore, archbishop of Canterbury, and Hadrian, abbot of its monastery, had established that great school in Kent, to which the English and the Irish had come flocking in crowds; when Aldhelm had labored over his Latin prose, his Latin riddles, in Wiltshire of Wessex; when, in the north, Bede had written of saints and sinners in his *History;* and Wilfred had built his churches; and Benedict Biscop had searched the Continent for books and paintings to enrich his abbeys; and Lindisfarne had brought forth its illuminated Book; when, later on, Alcuin had made his school of York famous wherever Latin words were learned.

But the fervor had died down when Aldhelm and Bede were dead and Alcuin had left his English school for Charlemagne and France. The old Benedictine spirit which had followed simple living and deep thinking in remote monastic cells during those earlier days was no longer meditating among books. The world was too much with monks and priests in England when the eighth century came toward its end. They had forgotten their Latin; many of them had never even learned the meaning of the words they chanted before the altar at Mass. If this was true of priests, what of the laity? Then the Vikings had passed over Lindisfarne and Jarrow, Bede's home, and Canterbury and York, to mar and to destroy their chapels and their libraries. Now, when Alfred had driven the Danes from his Wessex, when for a while there was peace, he hardly knew how he might try to stir a desire for learning into new life throughout his land.

Of two things at least he was well assured: First, he, the king, must educate himself, for his own hunger's sake and, far more, for the encouragement of the older men who needed as he did to find what they had never found; for the cause of the younger men, to whom a happier fortune would offer a chance to learn. And, second, he must "seek outside his kingdom what he did not have within it": scholars and teachers for himself and for his people, young and old.

2

For his own instruction he called a teacher from Wales: Asser, the man who was to write Alfred's *Life.* Asser was a priest from the community of St. David's, in Pembrokeshire, renowned in the sixth century, in the "Age of the Saints," of David, Cadog, Teilo, and many more, as a congregation of austere and holy life and study. But by the year 886, in Celtic Wales as well as in Saxon England, zeal for monastic living and learning had sunk almost out of sight. Asser, it is true, looked upon St. David's as a "monastery" and upon himself and his brethren as monks; but neither word can be used here in any true monastic sense. Nor were the priests of St. David's men of any deep scholarship. Asser knew more than most. Indeed, he stood out among churchmen of his time clearly enough to reach the notice of Alfred. But even Asser wrote mediocre Latin. He had no sense of clear, concise style, and our unbounded gratitude to him for having given us this *Life* of the king, our delight in his enthusiasm for his king and pupil, are often overshadowed by our immense irritation at his swollen periods and their disordered arranging.

Alfred, however, wanted to become familiar with Latin, of which he knew only a little. He therefore sent word to Asser, asking him to leave Wales and make his home at the West Saxon court. Asser came to talk over the matter with the king, probably at the royal manor of Eastdean, near Eastbourne in Sussex. There he found, as he tells us, a kindly welcome and a generous offer. After much talk, and moved by Alfred's earnest desire, he promised to return to him in six months' time "with an answer which should be of advantage to himself and his brethren and also agreeable to the King."

For Asser's community of St. David's was in trouble, brought about by recent happenings in Wales. Rhodri Mawr the Great, king of the whole of Wales in the north and of not a little in the center and south, had now ended his stormy career. In 876 he had been defeated in a battle with invaders, doubtless Vikings, fought one Sunday on the Isle of Anglesey and recorded as "Sunday's Action" in Irish annals. Ireland had given him shelter for a while, but death had come from the hands of the English in 878 after his return home to Wales. Then his lands had been divided among his six sons, of whom we know best the eldest one, Anarawd, king of Anglesey and of Gwynedd in the north, and his younger brother, Cadell, lord of

Ceredigion. From this time onward the realms of other Welsh kings, in South Wales, were constantly threatened, either by one or other of the sons of Rhodri or by the men of Ethelred, ealdorman of western Mercia, raiding across the border. At last the worry of these attacks had become too great. The southern kings had fled to King Alfred and had placed themselves as vassals under his protection. Among them was Hyfaidd, king of Dyfed, in Pembrokeshire.

It was this Hyfaidd who had been bringing trouble on St. David's. He had consoled himself in his anger against the sons of Rhodri Mawr by riding to attack lesser prey. St. David's was in his kingdom. Repeatedly he had raided its estates; he had driven away the bishop of St. David's, a relative of Asser, with some of his priests, and had caused much trouble to Asser himself, who also held high authority among his brethren—one tradition, of uncertain standing, declares he was their bishop. Now, however, the enemy had himself been forced to yield allegiance to King Alfred. It seemed, therefore, to Asser and to his fellow-priests a thing of distinct interest to their community that Asser should be at the court of Wessex, within the presence and the friendship of Hyfaidd's overlord.

Asser's promised return to this court was delayed by illness; but at last he did come and declared that henceforth he would divide his time between Alfred's household and his own St. David's. In 887, on St. Martin's Day, the eleventh of November, Alfred began, with the patient help of this devoted teacher, slowly to pick out and translate words and sentences from the Latin Vulgate Bible and from other Latin books within his reach. Often, too, whenever he had some leisure time by day, or at night when he was wakeful, he would call to him Asser or some other of the scholars at his court and give himself the delight of hearing these Latin words read aloud and interpreted for him.

One of these hours Asser has described for us in detail:

We were sitting together, the King and I, in his room, talking of this and that, as usual, and I chanced to read some passage to him aloud. He listened very intently. Then suddenly he drew out from his pocket a little book and showed it to me. In it were written out the Offices of the Day and some other psalms and prayers which he had read as a young man. He always carried this book with him, he said. Now he asked me to copy out in it for him that passage I had just read. Then I gave great thanks to Almighty God (silently, of course) for this work of progress and enthusiasm from the King. But there was no room in his little book; it was entirely full of writing. I hesitated a moment, for I wanted to sharpen still further his desire. He kept on asking me. At last I said, "Would you like me to write it out separately, on another sheet? I don't know whether we shall find any more passages you will want, but if we do, we will write them, too." And he said, "Oh, yes, indeed." I was delighted and hurried off to make a notebook. The first entry in it was that passage he had wanted, and on that same day he made me write in the book three more. So we went on, day after day, talking and hunting up more passages which he liked, until the book was full from end to end, almost as big as a Psalter. The King called it his *Handbook*, because he was working on it day and night, and very ably, too. It gave him great comfort.

So Asser wrote. We can trace knowledge of this "Handbook" as late as the twelfth century, but unhappily no manuscript of it is now extant.

Alfred showed his gratitude to Asser by many gifts. Once, after Asser had been asking again and again for leave to return to Wales, and always to no purpose, he was even on the point of risking a quarrel with the king. He had now been in Wessex eight months, and he was longing to find out how things were going at St. David's. It was Christmas Eve of 887, a little after sundown, when the king suddenly sent for him. As he entered the room, Alfred gave him two letters. Inside there were catalogues of all the properties belonging to two monasteries, at Congresbury and at Banwell, in Somerset. Congresbury is near Yatton, between Bristol and Weston-super-Mare, and is recorded in tradition as the home of St. Congar, a British saint, also known in Cornwall and Wales and Brittany. The parish church of Badgworth, some ten miles from Congresbury, is dedicated to him. Banwell village, near Axbridge and Cheddar, is visited now for its caves. Neither "monastery" would have been recognized as such by St. Benedict of Nursia or by England's apostle, St. Gregory the Great. But now, "filled full of all good things," they were the king's Christmas gift to Asser, a gift not unusual to an individual in those days when even laymen often owned monasteries and enjoyed their revenues. The Christmas Eve was still more delightful to Asser when Alfred followed up his gift by a permission to go home to Wales.

Later on, the king gave Asser a bishopric, probably the episcopal charge of part of Devon and Cornwall in the wide diocese of Sherborne, Dorset; Asser was holding the see of Sherborne when he died, ten years after the death of Alfred. These were the greater gifts which Alfred gave him. In addition, Asser writes, there were "presents without number, made every day, of every manner of wealth. The reader would get tired, if I were to write them all down." There is something pathetic in the gratitude of this great king and warrior for the unflagging encouragement which helped him along as he spelled out his Latin, line upon line and clause upon clause.

3

In England, Alfred turned in his need of teachers to Mercia. The abbey schools of Mercia had fared well under King Offa, and in Mercia men of learning were still to be found. Of these, Alfred called four to his court: Athelstan and Werwulf, of whom we know little except that they became priests of his royal chapel; Plegmund, whom in 890 he honored by gift of the archbishopric of Canterbury; and Werferth, since 873 bishop of Worcester.

Plegmund has come down to us in tradition as a hermit of Cheshire. His name still lives in the parish of Plemstall, near Chester, once known as Plegmundstall or Plegmundsham. A well there bears his name. Fulk, whom we have seen as archbishop of Reims, wrote to Alfred of his joy that Canterbury had so good and devoted a bishop, "busy in cutting away with the sword of his tongue that most perverse following of heathen error still left among the English people." He wrote, also, to Plegmund himself, congratulating him on his zealous crusade against lust and wantonness, "which seem to be deep-rooted in the nation."

4

That the "heathen error," which Plegmund "with the sword of his tongue" tried to cut away, persisted in this ninth century of England together with much practice of "Christian" magic is undoubtedly true and may especially be seen in connection with the healing art of medicine. Very probably during Alfred's lifetime some curious researcher, now nameless, was already beginning to collect from various sources that most interesting assortment of prescriptions for sickness found in the *Lacnunga*, the "Book of Healings." Here we find mention of the poisonous breaths which come flying upon man from east and north and west; of the evil of the number nine; of the workings of foul fiends. He who is attacked by such will flee to "a prescription, written on a housel-dish, a paten, for the holy drink against elf-disease and temptation from a devil."

Similarly, in *Bald's Leechbook*, another collection of remedies, perhaps put together under the inspiration of Alfred himself, we find prescriptions for all kinds of bodily ills. Here is one:

Against flying poison and every poisonous swelling. On a Friday churn butter, made with milk from a cow or a hind of one single colour. Do not add water. Sing over this nine times a litany, nine times a Paternoster, and nine times the appointed words of incantation.

And here is another, even more complicated, "a drink for a fiend-sick man":

Take cockle, lupine, betony, cockspur-grass, hassock, flow-er-de-luce, fennel, lichen off a church, lichen off a crucifix, and lovage. Place all in clear ale. Sing seven Masses over the mixture, put in garlic and holy water, and drip drops of this into every drink which the patient takes. Let him sing the psalms *Beati immaculati* and *Exsurgat* and *Salvum me fac, Deus,* and then let him drink of this drink, from a church bell. After he has drunk, let the priest sing over him *Domine, Sancte Pater Omnipotens.*

We may remember that similar remedies were prescribed for sickness such as that which for long troubled King Alfred himself in his childhood and early youth. An interesting connection, indeed, is found between Alfred and this *Bald's Leechbook.* In it there are a number of recipes said to have been sent to Alfred by Elias the Third, patriarch of Jerusalem from about 879 to 907. These set forth the medicinal properties of balsam; petroleum; triacle (treacle, from the Greek *thēriakē*), a syrup once, so men said, made with flesh of vipers as an antidote against their venom, but afterward concocted from juice of plants for use against many ills, and here especially given to Alfred as helpful in intestinal trouble; and "white stone," chalk, a corrective for acidity. We know from Asser that this Patriarch Elias sent letters and gifts to King Alfred; and we have also a letter written by Elias to Charles the Fat in 881, a petition for money with which to rebuild churches.

Among these first four scholars called to Alfred's court, the name of Werferth is memorable in that he inaugurated the succession of translations of Latin classics into Anglo-Saxon which was the ultimate aim of Alfred's long self-discipline in learning. To learn was indeed in itself a joy, but to teach his people was the duty of a king. And so, while Alfred was still intent on his lessons with Asser, with Athelstan and with Werwulf, he proposed to this bishop, Werferth, the work of translating into Old English the *Dialogues* of St. Gregory the Great.

The choice of this as the first of a series for the people of Wessex was a natural one. St. Gregory had sent Augustine to preach the faith to heathen Saxons, from Canterbury, whence it had come to Wessex. And, second, these *Dialogues* are full of spiritual fairy stories: miracles of holy men, wrought by prayer upon beast and bird, upon dragon and snake. There are many adventures, too, with the "old enemy," Satan. Above all, there is abundance of sound and good teaching of the faith of the church. The book was, in fact, eminently calculated to attract and to interest the ignorant people whom Alfred wanted to enlighten.

St. Gregory the Great had been pope from 590 to 604 A.D., one of the greatest of all who have held the see of St. Peter. He encouraged his people boldly during the advance of the Lombards against Rome; he governed the church in all parts of the world of his day; he kept watch over bishops, monks, nuns, clergy, and secular officials, including those many stewards of the immense papal estates; he maintained the dignity of Rome against the patriarch of the church in the East; he cared for the sick and the poor of his city; he wrote letters in multitude to all sorts and conditions of men and women; he administered the sacraments and preached continually in his Cathedral; he kept in all strictness that *Rule* of St. Benedict to which he was bound by his vows; and somehow he found time as well to write books. His *Dialogues* were the solace of those moments of leisure caught now and then in his earlier years of papal office. We may date them about 593.

Werwerth translated them very literally from their Latin into his own Anglo-Saxon, with errors of his own making here and there. For him the chief difficulty was that there was no intellectual norm of Anglo-Saxon narrative at hand for the conveying of his original. There is hardly any evidence for native English prose before Alfred's time; one's mind in review thinks mainly of charters or of Bede's translating of the Gospel of St. John. Hitherto prose form must have been molded, so far as it was molded at all, by oral narrative of stories, of legends, of tradition. A long and painful progress uphill was to lead from the immature beginnings of written sentences, clauses, periods, in Alfred's time to the end of the tenth century and the art of Aelfric's style.

But now, just as in Gregory's Latin, written for the men of his own world, so in Werferth's awkward Anglo-Saxon story, put together for the people of English race—that people whom Gregory had so longed to bring from heathen darkness into light—the saint himself, Gregory the pope, was presented, sunk in his own trouble of spirit. At the beginning of the book he is shown, encompassed by contentions and worries of his world in Rome, intensely homesick for the peace and solitary hours of prayer which once had been his in his Monastery of St. Andrew on the Caelian Hill. Now English readers were to hear him lamenting to his deacon, Peter: "Most like am I to a crippled vessel that labors in the waves of a towering sea. Tossed am I by the tribulations of this world, beaten by storm of strong winds in the ship of my soul." His misery is deepened as he thinks of those good men who served God well amid the sorrows of their generations: "I behold their nobleness, their virtue, and think how I myself lie here, downcast and prone among these low, mean things of my life."

Peter remarks briefly that he does not himself recall such very holy men in Italy. How many, for instance, have been famed there for miracles? "Miracles!" answers Gregory. "It would take all day to tell them!" And then he begins his tales and adds the morals which point their telling.

Here, among so many people, we find again the nun who went into her convent's garden one morning and, for its fresh delight, bit into a lettuce, but alas! forgot to bless it first with the holy sign. Soon she was seized with horrid pain. Her sisters knew it was the devil at his work and sent posthaste for a certain holy Equitius. The Father ran all the way, praying as he went. When he came panting into the garden, the devil called peevishly to him out of the poor nun's mouth: "What have *I* done? I was merely sitting on a lettuce, and she came and ate me!" The holy man with great wrath bade him depart in the name of God. Which he did, never to return.

Here, again, is the priest, Severus, who was called to give the last sacraments to a dying man and just could not tear himself away from the joy of his work among his vines: "Only this little bit to finish, and then I really will go." And, when he did start on his way, he met messengers from the house: "Do not trouble now. He is dead." This dreadful news, of course, threw the Father into anguish of heart, and he cried aloud that he had murdered the soul he had neglected to confess. But the Lord in mercy sent back the departed spirit to earth for a week and then received it again cleansed and fortified by holy rite and intercession from the lips of the penitent priest.

Here are those wonderful stories of St. Benedict, from Gregory's second book. Once more we see the monk who could not say his Office until Benedict smote the little black devil who kept pulling him away from prayer. Here is the humble lay brother, no Roman but barbarian in race, whom Abbot Benedict himself sent to cut away brambles in the garden at Monte Cassino. In his zeal he hit out so fervently that the blade of his billhook flew off into a pond. It was, of course, the monastery's billhook; the poor Goth had no hope of recovering it from that deep pond, and he was miserable indeed. But what was depth of water against the prayers of Benedict? The handle drew its blade back to the surface, like the ax head rescued by the prophet Elisha; and the Father sent off his barbarian son with "See now! There it is! Now get to work and don't worry."

Here, too, is that well-known raven which at Benedict's order carried far away in its beak the poisoned loaf sent as gift by a jealous priest to remove from earth this holy monk. Here, too, we recognize the brother who found a snake curled up in the flagon of wine which he was to bring as a present to Monte Cassino and had hidden for his own enjoyment; the horse which belonged to a lady of wealth, and which was lent to a pope to ride, and after that distinction absolutely declined to carry a woman on its back; the young novice of high birth who was silently disgusted at having to hold a candle to light the father abbot at his supper and who to his horror heard Benedict suddenly say, "My son, go and think the matter out alone by yourself"; the woman who faithfully day after day offered the Holy Sacrifice for her husband in prison and who heard afterward that a little more freedom from bonds had been given him each time she went to Mass.

Above all, here again we find the Father's sister, St. Scholastica, sitting with her brother one calm and lovely evening over supper on that one day in every year on which he might visit her in her convent. To no purpose she begged him to stay the night, "that until morning we may talk together of the joy of heaven." Nothing, he declared, would induce him to be absent for a night from his monastery. She said no more but laid her head upon her hands on the table. Directly she lifted it, a deluge of rain broke all around, with peals of thunder and terrific flashes of forked lightning. St. Benedict's dismay was only equaled by his knowledge. "Almighty God forgive you, my sister!" he cried. "What *have* you done?"

She smiled and said, "Listen! *You* would not hear me when I asked you, and so I prayed to my Lord, and he *did.* Now go and leave me for your monastery, if you can!"

He could not, for the storm raged on. So all that night they stayed awake to tell each other of life in the Lord. Three days afterward, as Benedict stood looking out from his cell, he suddenly saw his sister's soul flying like a dove upward to that "hidden mystery." Then he "rejoiced at this great wonder and gave thanks to God in hymns and psalms of praise."

Of course King Alfred watched, read, and discussed with intense interest this work of translation, finished about 891. At its beginning Werferth placed a preface, evidently reflecting the words of his king:

I, Alfred, graced by the gift of Christ with the honor of kingship, have clearly understood and often from holy books heard declared, that there is great need for us, to whom God has given so high a place in earthly things, from time to time amid the care of this world to open and yield our hearts to the divine and spiritual law. And therefore I have sought and asked from my faithful friends that they write out for me from books of God the teaching here given concerning the ways and wonders of holy men; so that I, sharpened in spirit through admonition and love, in the midst of this earthly vexation may search out the things of heaven.

It was in keeping with the king's character that he sent out this book for the teaching of his people as one written for his own spiritual need. But his efforts for himself were only the beginning. The doctrine that knowledge is virtue was also necessary, he knew well, for those nobles whose sons were being taught in his own court, and he kept them busy. Did any one of them, Asser tells us, declare that he could not learn or study because he was old, or because his mind, so long asleep to books, was slow to work, the king commanded him to get one of these boys, or some other kinsman, or, if he had none, then one of his servants, free or slave, whom he had encouraged to learn, and make this son or kinsman or servant read aloud to him, at least from Anglo-Saxon books, whenever there was a moment to spare, by day or by night. Very sorry for themselves they sometimes were, these older men, brought back to school in their gray hairs. But Alfred had a passion for the poetry of his own tongue, the poetry his ancestors had loved; and what he judged good for himself was good and meet for all around him.

5

Two men, named Grimbald and John, who were constantly working with Alfred, came from the Continent at his request about the same time as Asser came from Wales, in 886 or 887. Grimbald was a monk and priest of the abbey of Saint-Bertin, at Saint-Omer, in the Pas-de-Calais, northern France, a monastery which was of great importance in the records of medieval Europe. Light is thrown on his coming to England by a letter sent to Alfred from the same Archbishop Fulk, whose correspondence was unending. Here Fulk begins a lengthy epistle by rejoicing in the Christian spirit and work for state and church in England of this king of the English. May Alfred's desire meet its goodly reward, he continues, and may peace be multiplied for kingdom and for people; "and may the order and the substance of the Church— which in many ways, as you say, have broken down, either through frequent invasion and assault of the heathen, or through long lapse of time, or through the negligence of the higher clergy and the ignorance of those under their rule—may these by your diligence and industry be repaired, ennobled, and enlarged."

Alfred is now seeking, the letter goes on, aid in this matter from the see of Reims, a remark which brings forth here detailed discourse on St. Remigius and St. Augustine, "first Bishop of the English." When this has run its course, we read of the gratitude of the archbishop for a gift from Alfred of English hounds for use against "the fury of wolves, of which among other scourges, brought on us by just judgment of God, our country is full." In acknowledgment of this courtesy he is glad to grant Alfred's special request that he would send Grimbald from the cathedral and city of Reims to England for the furthering of its work of conversion and pastoral care. Grimbald is now a priest and, as Fulk openly suggests, "a most proper and suitable candidate for a bishop's see." His departure is causing Reims very much pain, and he must be received in England with due honor. For this end let a delegation of secular nobles and dignities, of bishops, priests, and deacons, cross the Channel to escort him thither, and, first, to declare before a specially summoned convention of the whole church of Reims that England will always hold Grimbald in the honor proper to his standing and character; to state further that it is the desire and unbreakable resolve of English ecclesiastics to keep all their days the canonical decrees and rulings of the church, as handed down from apostolic times, and as they shall be expressly set forward by the writer, Fulk himself, at this convocation in Reims. Further enlightenment in future days may, of course, be gained in England from Grimbald, well trained under Archbishop Fulk. It would be well, also, that, before leaving Reims, Grimbald should receive consecration as bishop from the hands of this archbishop in his own cathedral. Finally, should any in England, moved by the devil, rise in rebellion or dispute against this most honorable and learned Father, it will be for King Alfred in every manner to repress and curb such "barbaric ferocity."

Grimbald proved to be of very different character from that suggested by the archbishop's letter. He was content to serve Alfred and his purpose of education; to accept from the king residence with a few other priests in a little *monasteriolum* at Winchester, a clergy-house, certainly no Benedictine cloister; to decline, it would seem, the king's offer of the archbishopric of Canterbury, made to him in 889 before it was made to Plegmund; and to remain all his days a simple priest. Asser speaks of him as "a man truly deserving of respect, an excellent singer, right well learned in all Church and canon law and in Holy Scripture, endowed with all good morals and manners."

It was in connection with Winchester that Grimbald's fame for holy living grew in later days. There Alfred toward the end of his life greatly desired to build another, a New Minster, beside the Old Minster, the Cathedral of St. Peter, built in the seventh century. The king did not live to fulfil his purpose, his vow, as men declared it. But the enthusiasm and energy of Grimbald encouraged his son, Edward the Elder, to bring his thought to action in the early years of the tenth century. We read that upon Alfred's death Grimbald asked leave of Edward to return to France, but that Edward induced him to stay at Winchester by promising to build this second church and minster.

Here, and throughout England, Grimbald was honored as saint after his death on the eighth of July, 901. The day is already found marked as that of his feast in a Wessex church calendar of the tenth century, and by the end of the eleventh its observance was widely spread. We still have the Offices for his Day as recited at Hyde Abbey, Winchester, complete with twelve lessons describing his life.

The high-minded Archbishop Fulk of Reims in a letter to Pope Formosus described the people who lived around Saint-Omer, where Grimbald's abbey was located, as "barbarous in their talk," which meant that their speech was too Saxon and Germanic for his softer Frankish manner. Since Alfred was not sufficiently at home in Latin, when Grimbald arrived about 887, to converse freely with him in that language, the king must have been grateful for his Saxon tincture, akin to Alfred's own West Saxon speech. The other scholar from abroad, John, was himself a Saxon, of the "Old," the Continental race, so that John, the Old Saxon, could talk fluently with the English, West Saxon king.

John, nevertheless, was to have a hard time in England. We do not know much concerning his life before he arrived, about the same year as Asser and Grimbald. Asser described him as "priest and monk, a man of very keen mind, deeply versed in literary scholarship and writing, with skill in many other forms of art." It has been suggested that he came from the monastery of Corvey, or New Corbie, in the diocese of Paderborn, West Germany, a daughter house of the famous abbey of Corbie near Amiens in France. From Corvey many missionaries went forth, including that St. Anskar who preached to the Scandinavians. But this thought of Corvey as John's abbey is only a conjecture.

Alfred made John abbot of his new monastery at Athelney in Somerset. This, as we have seen, lay solitary in the midst of swamp and marsh. Asser, who knew it well in Alfred's own time, tells us that it could be reached only by boats or by one bridge, built between two towers at great cost of time and effort, and that the tower at its western end was well fortified and of especially beautiful work. The king himself was always craving leisure for quiet meditation, and he had thought that the solitude of Athelney would appeal to many who delighted in peace, alone with God and their books.

In this thought he was entirely wrong. In the present lapse of monastic zeal and work, novices could not be found to follow the discipline of such monasteries of Wessex as even after the wars were still standing, still fit for habitation, nearer the world of men. It proved impossible to fill this house at Athelney, damp, completely cut off among the alders of the forest, and surrounded by floods. Some priests and deacons came from the Continent, glad of refuge from Viking terror; some, too, of course, did come for the sake of its regular hours of prayer. But much of Alfred's new community consisted of children from Frankish lands, young enough for the training in religious life under such conditions. Among these was a boy from a heathen country whom Asser himself saw there, "and he was not the least among them, either." Perhaps, it has been thought, this was Oda, the Dane, who was educated somewhere in England and eventually, in 940, became archbishop of Canterbury; or, perhaps, Osketel, also of Danish race, archbishop of York from 950 to 971. The suggestions are interesting, entirely uncertain, but not impossible in matter of date, since Asser did not die, according to the *Anglo-Saxon Chronicle*, until 909.

John, it seems, was very firm in administering the rule of his isolated monastery. At any rate, an occurrence came to pass in the abbey which, as Asser described it, was "worthy of all hatred, contempt, and punishment." Two of its community, a priest and a deacon, both of Frankish origin, were moved by Satan and his envy to so great bitterness of mind against this man, their abbot, that they even made plans against his life. To this end they bargained with two Frankish servants of the house to kill him in the dead of night, when he made a practice of secret devotion in the monastery's little church.

One night, then, as John was kneeling before the altar, the two hired ruffians, with swords stolen for the purpose, rushed upon him. But the abbot was not only a monk trained in obedience and holy rule. "He was always quick and sharp of action, and—as I have heard [so Asser writes]—he knew something of fighting, and would have made a good soldier if he had not been keen on a better profession." He had heard these men creeping in, even before he saw them, and he had at once suspected that they were not entering for prayer. Now he boldly closed with them, shouting that they were no men, but devils. He was badly wounded, however, before any of his brethren came to help him. The noise of the struggle, of course, woke every one up in that tiny place, and most of them were terrified when they heard the abbot shouting "Devils!" Before they could reach the church, the two Franks had escaped to hiding in the forest. John was found lying half-dead upon the floor. He recovered, but we know nothing of his life in after years or when he died.

It is, however, pleasant to think of him and his six fellow-scholars, from Wales, from Mercia, from Continental lands, sitting often with Alfred to read aloud to him the Latin which he so longed to know, to aid and guide the king as he bravely stumbled across the arid plains of Latin grammar on his way toward the Delectable Mountains of Latin thought.

CHAPTER SEVEN

King Alfred AND THE LATER WAR AGAINST THE DANES, 892–96

SINCE 886 there had been peace from Viking war in England. But not in France or in Germany. For a moment, then, we must look at the continued assaults of the Danes on the Continent; for they are the prelude to Alfred's renewal of battle in his last great struggle against this common enemy.

Charles the Fat, as we saw, had lost his throne through his lack of courage and decision in face of these invaders. That had happened in 887; and as he had been king of the Franks of both West and East, that is, in both France and Germany, the nobles of these countries now debated and quarreled over the vital matter of succession. The powerful Fulk, archbishop of Reims, was, as ever, eager for the upholding of the Carolingian House; but this was represented at the time only by a boy eight years old, known in later years as Charles the Simple. Amid so many problems and contentions a child could not hold the crown; and, therefore, Frankish rule was now divided, as it had been before the reign of Charles the Fat. For Germany its nobles in 887 elected as king one Arnulf, of direct descent in the Carolingian line of Louis the Pious but of illegitimate birth. Illegitimate or not, as possessed of Carolingian blood, he held the advantage over the man, of noble but not of Carolingian birth, crowned in 888 to rule France: Eudes, that count of Paris who had fought for his city in the Viking siege of 885–86.

Eudes was welcomed to his throne with great enthusiasm, even though from the beginning of his reign many of his subjects disliked this departure from their royal tradition. It was, however, his failure to defeat the Danes which especially injured his chance of success. At first, on the twenty-fourth of June, 888, he "gained no little glory" by a victory over these invaders at Montfaucon, between the Aisne and the Meuse, not far from Verdun. His fellow-king, Arnulf, welcomed him at Worms with marked hospitality, and the powerful Baldwin, count of Flanders, promised to be his man. Later in the year we find the Danes on the Marne, besieging and burning the walls of Meaux. The next year, 889, they were ravaging Burgundy and Aquitaine, and in the autumn they marched upon Paris. There Eudes made a courageous stand, but was finally forced to pay ransom for his city. In 890 they were on the Oise, laying waste the land around Noyon. From thence in 891 they raided as far as the Meuse and were making their way back to their camp at Noyon when Eudes faced them again, near Valenciennes. Another victory like that of Montfaucon was his hope; but the Danes fled from him through the forest and regained their base. No greater success met him in another attempt, at Amiens; and, finally, late in the year, they fell upon him in an unguarded hour near Saint-Quentin and put him to flight.

Arnulf, on the other hand, began badly and ended well. His men pursued the Danes across the Scheldt and on the Meuse, but in an encounter of June, 891, they lost many nobles, secular and ecclesiastic, with much valuable equipment. When this was reported to Arnulf, then in Bavaria, his anger, his wounded pride, it was said, drove him to summon to his standard every soldier he could assemble, to cross the Rhine, and to settle his camp near the Meuse, with firm purpose of attack. The invaders, elated by their recent victory, marched on as usual, bent on plunder. Before long they found that Arnulf's army was coming to meet them, and they promptly established themselves, still confident of their power, behind a rampart of earth and timber on the bank of the river Dyle, near Louvain. "There, shouting insults and laughing in contempt, they called out to Arnulf and his troops to think of La Gueule, where the King's men had met their recent defeat, to remember that cowardly flight, those losses, soon to be theirs a second time. Arnulf in a rage ordered his men off their horses for a rush upon the barricade. Then there was a slaughter like to a massacre, and the Danes were laid low on the ground. Out of a multitude without number scarcely anyone was left to carry back word to the Viking fleet. Arnulf returned to Bavaria, full of gladness in his victory."

Thus Regino, at this time a monk of the monastery of Prüm, in the Ardennes, tells the story in his *Chronicle*. It was indeed worthy of note. History has looked back upon the battles of Edington, won by Alfred in England in 878, upon the determined defense of Paris in 885 by Eudes and Joscelin, and upon this victory of Arnulf by the river Dyle in Lotharingia on the first of November, 891, as the three outstanding records of Europe's resistance to the Vikings in this ninth century.

The battle of the Dyle brought an immediate joy to the Continent. In the autumn of the following year, 892, after a vicious attack against the abbey of Prüm, marked by murder and seizure of many of its monks, the Viking host returned to its fleet and set sail across the Channel for England. Now at long last France and Germany were released from the terror which for forty years had held them in its grip.

2

The main army of the Danes sailed in two hundred and fifty ships from Boulogne, carrying horses on board, and landed at the mouth of the little river Lympne, in eastern Kent. From there they pulled their boats upstream, a distance of four miles, until they reached the forest of the Weald. At Appledore they came upon a partly built fortress, occupied by a few peasants. These they turned out and took over the building, such as it was, for their own use. During this same year another Danish fleet of eighty ships sailed to the mouth of the Thames and settled its men at Milton Royal, on the bank of the Swale between Sheppey and the Kentish coast. They were commanded by the Viking chieftain Haesten, already well known for his prowess in raids on the Continent.

Alfred was faced by two dangers: that these two pirate

forces would unite and—far more serious—that the Danes of East Anglia and of Northumbria would come to help them. He had not forgotten that year of 884–85, when those in East Anglia under Guthrum "had broken peace" with him to give support to raiders from across the sea. He therefore exacted oaths from the Danes settled in both regions, and from East Anglia six hostages as well, in pledge of loyalty to their covenant. They all swore readily, and as readily broke their word, either by joining these new invaders in their sallies in quest of plunder and new land or in taking advantage of the situation to make raids on their own account. The king met the danger of a union between the two new Danish camps by placing himself and his army at a point between Appledore in the forest and Milton on the coast within easy reach of both. Thus he would be directly at hand should word of any movement be reported.

Day by day, night by night, the Danes prowled through the forest, wherever they could find free way. Continually, Alfred's men stole out to surprise and to attack them. In accordance with his plan of alternating service and leave of absence, half of his available fighters were on duty, half were tending the fields at home. With Alfred was his friend, Ethelred, to whom he had intrusted the governing of English Mercia. At one time during these raids and counterraids a run of bad fortune brought Haesten, the Danish chief, to meet the two English leaders in parley, to yield to them his oath of peace, with hostages for its observance, and to give his two sons to Christian baptism under their sponsoring. As was often the custom of the Danes, he had brought these boys and his wife with him to England, hoping that they might find there a new home on conquered land. Alfred, on his side, gave to Haesten valuable gifts, in money and other possessions. Soon afterward Haesten moved himself, his men, and his warships from Milton to Benfleet on the Thames, in Essex.

It was now 893. Early in the year the great Danish host at Appledore sent their ships, also, to Benfleet, and then sallied out on a long march to Hampshire and Berkshire, raiding as they went the countryside of Wessex. On their way back eastward they met disaster at Farnham in Surrey from the hands of English swordsmen. Young Edward, eldest son of King Alfred, was in command. Now he and his men fought the Danes, defeated them, wounded their leader, seized the booty they had captured from English fields, and sent them running for their lives. In their path lay the Thames. There was no time to look for a ford. They swam or floated across as best they could, carrying with them their helpless chieftain, and then fled up the bank of the Colne to one of the little islands in its course, near the modern village of Thorney, Buckinghamshire. Prince Edward followed fast upon their heels. When he caught up with them at Thorney, he at once threw around the islet a blockade, aided by Ethelred of Mercia, who had come from London to join him. For a while the Danes held out, hoping somehow to escape. Loyalty hindered them, for they would not forsake their leader, and they could not carry him farther in the haste of flight. At last, therefore, they gave way, offered hostages, and promised to leave Wessex land if they might depart freely and unharmed.

This was not to Edward's liking; but he was not himself at the time in any position to refuse. Many of his men, under the ruling of Alfred, were due for leave at home; and his store of food was almost at an end. So the Danes gladly made off, some to their fellow-countrymen in East Anglia, the greater number to Haesten and his base at Benfleet.

King Alfred had meant to come to the support of his son. Just as he was on his way, however, word reached him that these Danes of East Anglia, with those of Northumbria, had sent out two fleets to make a diversion and to hamper the fight of Wessex against Haesten. One of these fleets, a hundred vessels strong, sailed south to land its men for a siege of Exeter; the other, of forty ships, purposed blockade of a stronghold, also in Devonshire but on its north coast, facing the Bristol Channel. The king had at once turned for Exeter.

3

He was still in the west of England when cheerful news reached him. His son Edward and his ealdorman of English Mercia, Ethelred, had naturally been vexed at their failure to conquer those Danes on Thorney Island. Now, as summer set in, in 893, they gathered all the men available, including volunteers from the citizens of London and reinforcements from the west country, and marched boldly upon the main Danish camp at Benfleet. Haesten was away, plundering English Mercia, the land governed by that Ethelred who had shown him kindness. In an utterly determined attack the English army stormed Benfleet's defenses, captured them, drove out the Danes concentrated there, and seized all they had, women and children, armor, cattle, and movable property. All this treasure they carried off exultantly to London. Those of the ships which they could not take with them, to London or to Rochester, they hammered to pieces and burned in a great bonfire. Among the captives were the wife of Haesten and those two sons lately baptized in Alfred's presence. These Edward singled out and sent in triumph to his father. But the king remembered that he and Ethelred had received the boys from the font as godchildren and had prayed for them all good things. He sent them back with their mother to Haesten safe and unharmed.

This new success put fresh life into the English army. Haesten, however, again showed himself an ungrateful soldier. Now an immense army of Danes, all the invaders who had been at Benfleet, with very many from East Anglia and Northumbria, mustered at Shoebury on the coast of Essex near Southend-on-Sea, making ready for an arduous march. Along the course of the Thames they went, in this summer of 893, across Berkshire, Wiltshire, and Gloucestershire, to the river Severn. On its bank they built a camp at Buttington, in Montgomeryshire, near the Shropshire border.

The English on their part did not sit idle. "Then gathered Ethelred, ealdorman of Mercia, and Ethelhelm, ealdorman of Wiltshire, and Ethelnoth, ealdorman of Somerset [whom we have seen with Alfred at Athelney, and in Wedmore, host at Guthrum's 'chrism-loosing'], and the King's thanes, both those at home and those on duty in fortresses, from every walled town east of the river Parret in Somerset, from every walled town east and west of Selwood, from every walled town north of the Thames, from every walled town west of the Severn, with some chieftains of the Welsh." Alfred could not come. He was held in Devonshire, watching and wearing down the attempts of the enemy there.

The great English army under Ethelred, however, pursued the Danes to the Severn and set to work with energy in throwing up siege ramparts around the Danish camp. For many weeks the blockade went on, while food within steadily diminished and hunger began to press. At last the Danes had killed and eaten almost all their horses. Nothing remained for them but to surrender or to try to make their escape. And escape by cunning strategy they did, although many of them were killed in the attempt. Those who got away reached somehow their base and their ships at Shoebury. History has not given us the details of this bold and resolute retreat across the English Midlands, of men worn by fighting and by famine, defeated, wounded, lacking necessary supplies of food, surrounded by enemies, entirely dependent on a chance of plunder or on help from fellow-Danes settled along their way.

Yet not even this experience quenched the Viking spirit or the hope of gaining further permanent settlement in England. This same year of 893, in early autumn, these invaders drew again to their aid another multitude of their countrymen from East Anglia and Northumbria, left their wives and children, ships, and other precious possessions in East Anglia, and marched without a stop, day and night, northwest along the old Roman road of Watling Street, into Cheshire. Once there, before the

English, again following with all haste, could overtake them, they shut themselves off behind the walls of the deserted Roman city of Chester.

Then Ethelred and his fellow-leaders arrived with their army before those walls and ordered a siege as thorough as they could devise, far more drastic that that of Buttington. They posted men on unbroken watch in the hope of catching and killing any Dane who crept out to find food. They carried off all the cattle they saw throughout the countryside, sent their own horses to graze down the fields, and burned over all the scanty provender still left standing.

Once more the Danes knew themselves beaten. Once more they managed to break out from behind the English blockade, this time to move across the border into Wales and to stay there some nine months, living on what they could seize. Then, in the summer of 894, they marched across England again, taking devious roads through Danish territory to elude the English and to get food from Danish sympathizers. At last they were again in Essex and went to settle on Mersea Island, off the Essex coast.

But not for long. Even before the winter of 894 was upon them, their restless spirit had driven them out again to find new hunting grounds, to draw their ships up the Thames, then onward up its tributary, the Lea. In this river they moored their ships, built on its bank another fortified camp some twenty miles from London, and settled down to wait, doubtless in the hope of a general Danish uprising and the return of London itself into Danish hands.

From London English fighters poured out to dislodge them and failed; the enemy remained on the Lea until the summer of 895. Then Alfred, who by this time had relieved the city of Exeter from its long siege, arrived to protect the harvest and the reapers in the fields around this enemy, to keep these pirates from foraging, and in the end to drive them away. He had decided that the best plan was to dam up the course of the river and thus to cut off from the Danish ships all chance of escape. Directly the Danes realized what he had in mind, they abandoned their ships and fled. Another long march took them west across the Midlands, once again to the Severn, to encamp for the winter of 895–96 on its bank at Bridgnorth, in Shropshire. They marched now the more swiftly because they had left their women and children, who had been with them on the Lea, again in the care of the East Anglian Danes.

4

Bridgnorth was their uneasy home until the summer of 896. Then finally they gave up hope. For them there was, it now became clear, under Alfred and his ealdormen generals, no possibility of gaining new land in England for lasting settlement and possession. At all events, they could only wait upon the future; at the moment only the lands already Danish could be theirs. They broke camp and went their different ways: some to mingle with their own people, in Northumbria or in East Anglia or in Danish Mercia; others back across the Channel, to raid once more on the Seine.

The *Anglo-Saxon Chronicle* ends thus its record of this

time: "The Danish host, thank God, had not utterly broken England. The English people were far more afflicted during these three years by pestilence, falling alike on cattle and on men; and, especially, in that many of the King's thanes, and the most excellent in the land, died during this time: Swithwulf, bishop of Rochester, and Ceolmund, ealdorman of Kent, and Beorhtwulf, ealdorman of Essex, and Wulfred, ealdorman of Hampshire, and Ealheard, bishop of Dorchester, and Eadwulf, the King's thane in Sussex, and Beornwulf, reeve in Winchester, and Egwulf, the King's marshal, and many others. But these were the most distinguished."

One more happening remains to be noted here, yet one of great importance. In this same year of 896 the warships of those Danes settled in England were continually bringing their crews to land for raids along the coast of Wessex. This brought Alfred sharply to realize that the England governed by him must have a fleet which could meet the enemy on the sea with better chance of success than heretofore. He thereupon ordered warships to be made, "nearly twice as long as those of the Danes, and swifter and steadier and higher, some with sixty oars, some with more; not built after the Frisian manner nor after the Danish, but as seemed best and most useful to the King himself."

These new ships were not the success for which he had hoped, although they were in action the same year against six Danish vessels attacking the Isle of Wight and the coast of Devon. Perhaps the description given above, also from the *Anglo-Saxon Chronicle*, is somewhat too optimistic. Undoubtedly, their navigators and oarsmen suffered through lack of experience in managing boats of this size. Nine of them ran aground at this time. Nevertheless, although two of the Danish ships escaped, two were seized, and their men killed on the spot; and two were so damaged that they were driven upon the Sussex coast. All on board were at once captured and taken to Alfred's court, then at Winchester. The king had them all hanged.

It is in the building of English ships, however, whatever their fate, that the interest lies; for in this enterprise of Alfred we may see the earliest beginnings of the British navy.

5

The wars of Alfred's reign in England were over. There remained some "discord" between English and Danes in the north, a trouble still festering in 899, the year of Alfred's death, and of natural concern to Wessex. In general, however, during his last years, from 896 onward, there was a lull, destined to last until the reign of his son Edward the Elder. About 893 Anarawd, king in North Wales, and his brothers with him, deserted the Danes of Northumbria, their allies for a while, and Anarawd came to Alfred, seeking peace and friendship. The king welcomed him with marked courtesy, rejoiced to see him receive from the bishop the laying-on of hands in confirmation, gave him many gifts, and accepted his homage as ruler in Wales under his own overlordship on the same terms as those governing Ethelred in English Mercia.

CHAPTER EIGHT

King Alfred AND HIS EARLIER TRANSLATIONS

IN THE LAST TWELVE years of his life, from 887 until 899, the king was giving all the time he could spare from the campaigns of war and the burden of government to his work of enlightening the ignorance of his people, of making books available to them in their own language. This labor was, indeed, furthered and eased by his learned friends. Yet much of it was to be done by himself, carried out in his own way, in words chosen by himself, and with an increasing desire for his independence not only of these counselors but, as time went on, of the very originals which he undertook to translate.

We do not know the exact date of any one of the six translations from Latin writers of earlier medieval centuries—fourth, fifth, sixth, eighth—which were made either by Alfred himself or by others in constant consultation with him and under his eyes; but scholars of modern times have arranged them in a highly probable order. The first was that book of Werferth, the translation of St. Gregory's *Dialogues*. Next, as we may think, followed another translation from the thought of this same saint. This time, however, the work undertaken was no collection of tales, nor was it intended for Alfred's unlearned people at large. It was an Anglo-Saxon version of Gregory's *Cura Pastoralis* (*Pastoral Care*).

This *Cura Pastoralis* was a manual of instruction for the bishops of the church in the sixth century, the rulers and the shepherds of their people, written by Gregory soon after he became pope in 590. The pope's work here falls into four parts. First, he analyzes the motives which draw men of differing types to offer themselves for the great office of bishop of souls, the perils and temptations which await them. Then he holds up as in a mirror the ideal bishop, describing what kind of man should, and what kind of man should not, be set apart for a bishop's work. In the second part he pictures the life which this bishop should lead: his inner devotion to prayer and solitude; his love for all his charge; his stand upon the rock of his faith, where, guided by the Spirit, he may turn, as need arises, to speech or to silence, to gentleness or to severity, to contemplation or to administration, to delight in God alone or in the busy caring for God's creatures. In Part III he gives a long list of the various characters with whom this bishop has to deal, together with the treatment he should give to each: men and women, rich and poor, happy and sad, high and low of rank, intelligent and stupid, bold and timid, generous and envious, well and sick, silent and garrulous, zealous and lazy, greedy and self-denying, proud and humble. His book closes with the return of this ideal bishop from his outward adventures into the depths of his own heart, there to mourn his failings, to remember that a bishop is on earth a mortal man, and to try to imagine himself as he appears in the eyes of God. Its last words are addressed by Gregory to "John," probably the archbishop of Ravenna, at whose request this *Pastoral Care* was written: "You see, my friend, that, as your censure drove me to it, I have labored to show what sort of man a shepherd of souls should be. I have painted a goodly man, I who myself am foul. I, who direct others toward the shore of perfection, am still tossing and turning in the surge of my sins. I beseech you, in the shipwreck of this life, uphold me by the plank of your prayer."

This Latin original had been well known in England in former years. St. Augustine of Canterbury had brought it with him from Rome to guide and console him when the same Pope Gregory the Great had sent him forth to preach to those "barbarous, savage, and unbelieving" English, whose very language he and his fellow-monks did not understand. In 734 the Venerable Bede, writing from his monastery of Jarrow to Egbert, bishop, and afterward archbishop, of York, had given this counsel to his friend: "Study with diligence the words of the most holy Pope Gregory, his long and careful study of the life and the shortcomings of rulers of the church, so that your own words may always shine forth, seasoned with the salt of wisdom, rising above common speech, more worthy of the ears of Heaven." Alcuin, once head of the cathedral school of York, had written from France in 796 to another archbishop of York, his son in the faith, Eanbald the Second: "Wherever you go, let the Pastoral Book of Saint Gregory go with you. Read it very often; reread it, that you may see your own self and your work by its light, that you may hold before your eyes how you should live and teach. For it is a mirror of a bishop's life; it is medicine for all the wounds of the devil's deceit."

2

The version of this book of Gregory in the Anglo-Saxon of Alfred's people of Wessex was made by the king himself, after he had thoroughly studied and translated the Latin with his various teachers. His aim and his method here can best be understood through a translation of part of the Preface which he wrote for this Anglo-Saxon rendering:

King Alfred gives greeting to Bishop Werferth in these words, with love and friendship.

I want you to know that very often I think back on these things: what wise men there were formerly throughout England, both of religious and of secular calling, and what happy times those were; how the Kings who then held rule over this people obeyed God and His messengers; and how they not only kept peace and good custom and governing at home, but also enlarged their realm abroad; and what success was theirs both in battle and in wisdom.

I have called to mind, too, how eager in those days religious orders were for teaching and for learning and for all the services which were theirs for God; and how men from abroad came to seek wisdom and knowledge in this land; and how we now have to get such men from without, if we are to have them at all. So utterly has knowledge fallen away in England that when I began to rule there were very few men on this side of the Humber who could understand their [Latin]

Mass-books and Offices in English, or even translate a letter from Latin into English; and, I think, not many beyond the Humber. So few there were that I cannot even call to mind a single one south of the Thames. Thanks be to Almighty God that we have now any teachers in our land. . . .

On all this I thought, and I thought also how, before all was destroyed and burned, I saw the churches throughout England standing full of treasures and books. We had then a great multitude of servants of God; but very few of them knew what was in their books. Not one whit could they understand of these books, because the books were not written in their own native speech. . . .

When I thought on all this, I wondered very, very much why none of the good and wise men, who were once everywhere in England and had thoroughly learned their books, had not translated these into their own English. But soon I answered myself and said: "These scholars did not suppose that any men would be so careless and that learning would so fall away; and so it was their very desiring which stayed them from translation, because they wanted wisdom in our land to grow in greatness as we learned more of languages."

Then I bethought me how the Law [by which Alfred means, of course, the Old Testament] was first found in the Hebrew language, and how afterwards, when the Greeks learned it, they turned it all into their own tongue, and all other books, as well. And so, too, the Romans, after they learned it, turned it through skilled interpreters into their own speech. Yes, and all other Christian peoples translated some part of these books. Therefore it seems better to me, if you all also think it, that we, too, turn some books, those which all men need most to know, into that language which we all can understand. I think also that, very easily, if God aid us and peace be ours, we can bring it about that all the young men of England who are of free birth and have sufficient means and are not specially gifted for other work, be set to learning. After this wise: First, let them all learn to read English writing; then let those who should be taught more and to a higher degree study the Latin tongue.

When, too, I laid this to mind, how the knowledge of Latin had fallen away throughout England, and yet I knew that many people could still read English, then, busy as I was with many other and various cares of this kingdom, I began to turn into English the writing called in Latin, *Pastoralis*, and in English, *The Shepherd's Book*. Sometimes I translated word for word, sometimes sense for sense, as I learned it from Plegmund, my Archbishop, and from Asser, my bishop, and from Grimbald and John, my Mass-priests. First, I learned to understand the matter of it as clearly as I could, and then I turned it into English. And I shall send a copy of this translation of mine to every bishop's see in my kingdom.

3

Probably in 894 and onward, we are to imagine Alfred stealing his hours "of peace" for this work. The date is to a certain extent settled by the evidence of Alfred's Preface and of Asser's *Life* of the king. For in his ninety-first chapter Asser writes that Alfred had been troubled by sickness from his twentieth to his forty-fifth year, "the present time." This would date the *Life* in 893; and, as there is no mention in it of this, or of any other of the five translations that followed Werferth's version of Gregory's *Dialogues*, we may think that none of these was begun before late in 893 or afterward. Asser does mention Werferth's *Dialogues*, and he would surely have written with joy of this new plan of his king for further translations, and of their making, had they already been in preparation. If he had, he would, indeed, have saved students of Anglo-Saxon prose much trouble!

In this first of his own attempts Alfred was, of course, feeling his way. His translation of Gregory's *Pastoral Care* adheres closely, even awkwardly, to the original. Face to face with the Latin language and with Gregory's training in Latin rhetoric and style, with Gregory's power of expression, either complex and elaborate, or austere and concise, the immaturity of English prose writing at this time and Alfred's lack of experience and knowledge made simplicity and shortcoming inevitable. There are errors and misunderstandings of the Latin and deviations of thought, too, in this Anglo-Saxon version. The king read the *grassantur* of Gregory, which means "they walk about," as identical with the late Latin *crassantur*, or *grassantur*, "they grow fat." In the story of Saul, who cut off a piece from Samuel's robe and was himself condemned to be cut off from his kingdom, Gregory used the phrase "cut off" in its spiritual sense, Alfred in the material. Sometimes Alfred added words to explain Gregory's meaning, to make it a little more vivid for his Anglo-Saxon readers. "What is the use of enumerating all these things," wrote Gregory, "unless we briefly describe the methods by which each should be treated?" Alfred turned the question: "What is the use of naming the keys, unless we also in a few words show what they are keeping under lock?" The Latin original quoted from Proverbs in the Vulgate: "As deep water, so are the words of a [wise] man." Alfred pictured the thought in a more concrete image: "A very deep pool is dammed up in the wise man's mind." Gregory's bishop was "bound by the necessity of holding fast righteousness, since his is the honor of ruling a flock." Alfred wrote that "it is very needful for the bishop to be bound to righteousness with the rope of the understanding" of this honor. Sometimes the king in quoting passages from the Bible added a few words to tell his readers where, in which book, these were to be found. In general, throughout, by either adding or omitting, he translated Gregory's many texts from the Latin Bible in a simple and free manner.

These are only a few illustrations of Alfred's work in translation. For the student who is keen on comparisons, experts have made careful and copious lists of Alfred's additions, omissions, use of a pair of words instead of the original single one, changes in sentence construction, simplifying, and actual errors, both for this and for the other translations which are connected with the king's name.

More interesting, perhaps, to others than the philologist, is the thought that surely, as the king slowly plowed his way through these admonitions for the spiritual shepherds of his realm, he must often have been cheered or depressed as he looked into his own conscience in their searching light. For Gregory's words of counsel and of rebuke to his *rector*, "ruler," his bishop, would certainly come home to the mind of a Christian secular ruler, especially to such a king as Alfred. Those seven rules laid down by the pope for his bishops pointed truly toward those same ideals for which Alfred himself was striving in his own life and work:

That the ruler keep his body clean from sinful lusts;
That he be strong in the power of self-denial;
That he be filled with the sweetmeats of learning;
That he be patient with tiresome things and with all delay;

That he be ready and confident for the holding of rule;
That he be kind and courteous;
That he be stern and strict for the upholding of righteous-
ness.

Thus in Gregory's picture Alfred saw the ideal ruler, who was father of his people for their instruction, who was their mother in compassion. He must ever be working for his subjects, utterly loyal to them and their welfare, evenly poised, holding both their fear and their love. David, "God's darling," was a better man, according to Gregory, as a simple subject than as a king; for as king he slew his own true thane. Subjects, on the other hand, must so revere their lord that they slay him not even with the sword of their tongue; sin against one's lord is sin against God, who created the lord's office of rule. These thoughts of Gregory are, indeed, exactly the thoughts of King Alfred in his *Laws*.

Awful, continues the pope, in Alfred's translation, is the ruler's burden of responsibility. As an army fails in the battle when its general makes a mistake, so all the members of a body, even though they be in themselves strong and well, are useless when the head is sick. He who governs others must tread the middle path. It is God whom he must desire to please rather than men; and yet he must try to please his people also, that by their confidence in him he may lead them to love of their Creator. Gentleness and generosity must be his; yet sometimes gentleness is but a cloak for sloth and cowardice. Anger must control the stubborn offender; yet often a sinful passion of anger finds its excuse and is falsely held to be a boiling flood of righteous zeal. Sincerity is the hallmark of good rule. Did not Christ rebuke the Pharisees for tithing mint and dill and cummin, while they left untithed more valuable possessions? Mint and dill and cummin are, it is true, herbs of lesser value in gardens; but they send out strong fragrance. The man who seeks by fragrance of seeming virtue to hide his lack of worth resembles them.

The truly good ruler will be humble. "For humility was Saul raised above other men, and for pride he was cast down" from his kingly power, wrote the pope in Alfred's Latin model. Nebuchadnezzar, king of Babylon, for his boasting was made by God as one of the wild beasts that roam the field. "That man," declared Gregory, "will hold his power aright who is able alike to accept or to refuse it."

Whether bishop or king, a ruler often has charge over many lands, much wealth, and must answer to God for his using of these. Here, also, Alfred pondered as he translated St. Gregory's words by his own. "It is written in the books of Solomon that a man shall not say to his friend, 'Go, and come again tomorrow; then will I give thee something,' if he can give it to him rightly then and there." "The foremost injury a man can do to God is to do nothing for Him Who gave him all he has." "Give much, give little, as need and wisdom direct. And remember, too, not to indulge your generosity by useless waste. As it is said, 'Keep thine alms, and throw them not away.' "

Now and again the pope's words on sickness and pain of body must have comforted this king, continually, if we may believe Asser, troubled by illness and its fears: "So the Divine rule, before it gives a man skill and power, often shows his weakness and infirmities, lest he be unduly elated by these gifts."

St. Gregory's words on teaching, too, must on their part have awakened many echoes, set on foot many resolutions, in Alfred's mind. As the king bent over his Latin manuscript and wrung from it its English sense, his eye fell on certain phrases, surely, he must have thought, intended for such as he himself. Thus he rendered their meaning to him: "All holy teachers who now teach in the darkness of this world are like the cocks which crow on dark nights. And the teacher crows like the cock when he calls aloud, 'Now is it time for us to awake out of sleep.' So let the teacher first shake himself into wakefulness and beat himself with the wings of his thoughts. Then let him arouse other men to diligence of good works."

He who would teach, Alfred found in this book of the pope, must gird himself in preparation. So, in Alfred's words, declared the Preacher of the Old Testament: "Thou, young man, be not quick to call aloud and to teach, even though one ask thee twice. But do thou wait upon thine answer until thou know that thy speech hath both its beginning and its end." In other words, the teacher will himself draw from the well of his own learning before he pour out the water of knowledge "along the King's highway"; then shall each man who finds take thence, in his measure and after his power.

The art of teaching, in the well-known words of Gregory, is the "art of all arts." Why, then, he asks, and Alfred echoes him, do the unlearned dare to enter upon it? Does a doctor dare without due knowledge to attempt to care for sick bodies? Yet knowledge itself is only the first of the true teacher's needs. He only is truly skilled to teach who has acquired the power of patience. For patience is the nursing mother of all knowledge and all skill, "and every man is found so much the less learned than another as he is the more impatient."

Finally, for both pope and king, the ruler and teacher will so hold in his mind and in his hands the manifold duties of his charge that he suffer not the rising dust of these cares to dim his vision of the horizon beyond. Here, once more, his way on this earth must follow the middle, the crown of the road. He must never so lose himself in contemplation above this earth that he will not, that he cannot, come down from the mountain of his desire to tend the weak, the ignorant, and the sinful at his earthly door.

4

It is pleasant, and it is also reasonable, to think that Alfred turned from this effort for the instruction of his spiritual rulers to work again for the layfolk of Wessex, now to try to bring home to them in clear and simple form the story of the adventures, the perils and the marvels, of the Christian converting of their land from its heathen state. In this thought we might place here the translating into Old English of the *Church History of the English People*, a Latin work completed by its English writer, St. Bede, at his monastery of Jarrow in the Northumbrian county of Durham in the year 731.

This *History* was a fitting climax to the many writings of one who, in the words of the prayer laid before his altar and tomb in the Galilee Chapel of Durham Cathedral, "living his life in an obscure place, never ceased his diligence in prayer and in study." Here Bede told, in a Latin written in Anglo-Saxon England, but blessedly free from the complexities and tortuous windings in which Anglo-Saxon Latin is at times entwined, the doings of the saints and sinners who, as kings and queens, as bishops and priests, as monks and nuns, as ordinary people, succeeded one another in the annals of English life, from the days of St. Gregory the Great to this year, late in Bede's own lifetime. Alfred may well have longed to stimulate his English people of Wessex by bringing before them in their own language this record of heroic deeds, of battles and of days of endurance, of famine, fire, and sickness, suffered in England in the patience and boldness of Christ; of grievous sin and its defeating; of miracles beyond human understanding, yet seen of men; of visions of a Country beyond this earth and its common lot.

We still have this Old English version of the *History* of Bede. Its words and the manner of their using tell us that it was made in Alfred's time and that it was an early work in the series of the six translations initiated, or directed, or actually made by him. But who exactly was the author of this Old English translation is a question around which discussion has flowed from pens in varying languages, in England, on the Continent, and in America.

There is, indeed, written evidence for Alfred's own authorship. Aelfric, who came from Cernel, Dorset, to be abbot of the monastery of Eynsham in Oxfordshire early in the eleventh century, who was a scholar of repute, and who in his Anglo-Saxon writing looked back from the height of its achieving to Alfred's struggles at the foot, wrote in his *Sermon on Saint Gregory* that Alfred turned this *History* from Latin into English. So, in the twelfth century, did William, monk of Malmesbury Abbey in Wiltshire; so does a manuscript of this Old English version, belonging to Cambridge University and attributed to the eleventh century.

On the other hand, students of Anglo-Saxon in its varying forms have protested that all this tradition, coming from a later time, may well have sprung from Alfred's repute rather than from the fact of his translating. They have pointed out the undoubted presence, in extant manuscripts of this translation, of many words and forms of words belonging, not to the West Saxon dialect of Old English which was Alfred's, but to the Anglian dialect of Mercia, of the English Midlands. Hence it has been thought that very probably this version was originally made by one of Alfred's scholars from Mercia, more especially, by that Werferth, bishop of Worcester, who made the translation of St. Gregory's *Dialogues*.

Those who have leaned toward King Alfred as author have argued that perhaps his West Saxon original was lost; that our copies spring from one made by a Mercian hand; or that two original versions were made, one in Anglian, another in West Saxon dialect; or that Alfred's West Saxon translation might have been revised in places by one of his Mercian scholars.

Those who hold that Alfred was not the author, on the other hand, have seen a likeness between this version of the Bede and the work of Werferth in the Old English *Dialogues*. They have found in the many "word-pairs"— renderings of one word of the original Latin by two in the Anglo-Saxon translation—not a simple desire for explanation, but a skill in reflecting the Latin art of rhythm, resembling that of Werferth and totally different from the style of Alfred's translation of the *Pastoral Care*. They have thought to see a partiality for the north in the treatment of Bede's material here; and they have remarked on the rather surprising failure to add to Bede's book more detail concerning the church history of Wessex, Alfred's own kingdom. They have declared the exceeding closeness of this translation to its Latin original to be out of accord with Alfred's growing desire to add observations of his own.

Unfortunately, evidence from Anglian texts for purposes of comparison is limited, and the matter remains unsettled. It has seemed worthwhile thus briefly to indicate the problem here; but it need not worry us unduly. We shall not stray far from the truth if we believe that the *Church History of England* by the Venerable Bede was translated into Anglo-Saxon, if not by Alfred himself, then, at his bidding and with his constant co-operation, by one, or perhaps by several, of his scholars. Among these, as we have seen, those from Mercia held a leading place.

Errors are not lacking in the translation; but the chief point of interest in regard to the use of Bede's Latin material by the translator or translators is that about one-quarter of it is here omitted or greatly cut down. Especially, a number of papal letters are not found in the Anglo-Saxon version, and much information about Pope Gregory the Great is lacking. Poems in honor of saints are also omitted and details of the difference, in regard to the dating of Easter, between the Celtic church of Britain and the English church which obeyed Rome. The reason for these omissions was probably a fear of wearying simple minds in England by documents and discussion of little interest to them, of stretching out this *History* into too great length. As for the schism between the Celts and Rome, that, by the time of this later ninth century, had long been healed through the general adoption of Roman practice in this as in other matters of discipline.

Those who read Anglo-Saxon will do well to enjoy in this at least "Alfredian" book the familiar story of St. Gregory's yearning over the English boys, "not Angles but angels," whom he saw standing for sale at the hands of slave-dealers in the market place of Rome. The narrative ends thus: "Soon afterward, when he was Bishop, he carried out the work which he had long willed, and sent hither to Britain holy teachers, of whom we spoke before. And he, Saint Gregory, with his exhortations and his prayers helped to bring it about that their words should be fruitful for the will of God and the good of the English people." They should read also the story of the debate in Northumbria of its King Edwin and his counselors on the great question of the allegiance of their people, whether it should be given to the heathen deities they had revered so long or to this new and strange Christian God; and of the counsel offered by one of these nobles to his king: "Thus seems to me, O King, this present life of man on earth in comparison with the time which is unknown to us. It is as if you sat at supper with your ealdormen and thanes in wintertime, and the fire were kindled, and the hall warm, and it rained and snowed and stormed without. Then came a sparrow and swiftly flew through the house, and entered through one door and went out by the other. In truth, while he is inside, he is not struck by the winter storm; yet this is but a glancing of an eye and the briefest moment of time; and soon he comes again from winter into winter. So also this life of man appears for but a little while; what goes before or what follows after, we know not. Therefore, if this new teaching bring aught more sure or more seemly, it is good that we should follow it." And, finally, the story of the humble Caedmon, who tended the cows in obedience to St. Hilda for her monks and nuns at Whitby on the coast of Yorkshire, who sang for all men at an angel's bidding of the glory of God in the creation of his world and died "very blithe of heart" in his love of his brethren and of all God's souls.

The Anglo-Saxon version, whether or not the actual work of Alfred, is in these ancient and familiar stories not unworthy of the Latin of the great Bede himself.

CHAPTER NINE

King Alfred AND HIS LATER TRANSLATIONS

ALTHOUGH, as I have said, we cannot be certain of the order and time of translating these various works, it is once more reasonable to think that Alfred turned from instructing his people of Wessex in the church history of their own England to teaching them something of the past history of their world as a whole. This time, indeed, and from this time onward, we may safely hold him himself as the translator.

His original he found in the work of a Catholic priest, possibly born in Spain, but far more probably in Portugal. This priest's name was Paulus Orosius. He lived and wrote in the early years of the fifth century after Christ; and he was a devoted follower of the great St. Augustine of Hippo in North Africa.

In these 400's of our era the Roman Empire throughout its vast extent, from the Tiber to the Rhine and the Danube, and among the peoples of the Mediterranean, was suffering from those barbarian invasions which preceded and prophesied its fall in the West, from massacres and plunderings and plagues unnumbered. Naturally its citizens, of whom so many still stoutly adhered to the pagan faith of their ancestors, were declaring that these manifold and terrible visitations were being brought on them through the wrathful vengeance of the gods of ancient Rome, who would not brook their supplanting by the new worship of one named Christ. Augustine, therefore, who himself was preparing an answer to this pagan fallacy in his *City of God*, requested Orosius to write by way of supplement a narrative, as Orosius describes it, "based on all the histories and annals available, of all the grievous wars, foul epidemics, baneful times of famine, ghastly earthquakes, unheard-of floods, fearful conflagrations, savage blasts of lightning, storms of hail, wretched murders and crimes" which had descended on men in past heathen ages. This persuasive story, at Augustine's bidding, was to be "brief and well-ordered."

Orosius was delighted at the task. Here was an honor given him by his beloved master; here was a work for the church and for the heathen whom he longed to convert; here was business of much research. He set to with all his might and by the year 418 had produced *Seven Books of History against the Pagans*, books crammed with details, bristling with names of peoples, persons, and places in almost every paragraph, and punctuated by exhortations: "See now, you heathen, and believe, you who jeer at our present Christian age, so far happier than the past!"

The narrative ran from the earliest times of which Orosius could find knowledge to his own century. It became a classic in the earlier Middle Ages, a textbook for Christian readers of history. To Alfred it was an obvious, even an ideal, choice; but it also offered to him an undertaking of almost insuperable difficulty. After the comparatively clear and simple Latin of St. Bede, after the ordered, if "unclassical," periods of St. Gregory the Great, he now faced the diffuse Latin flood poured out by Orosius, bearing, as it swept along, its swirling burden of facts, or at least what Orosius regarded as facts.

The king of Wessex, however, true to his nature, was undaunted. From this seething mass he made in his Anglo-Saxon a story written in as simple and popular, as clear and direct, a style as he could devise, hoping thereby to descend to the level of his uninstructed readers. Many names he recast in an English form. Roman terms he explained, as, for instance, when the Roman vestal virgin becomes "a nun" and Roman cohorts are described as "what we now call *truman*," or troops. The errors of Orosius did not concern Alfred; indeed, he makes hair-raising mistakes of his own. Names are continually misspelled by him; persons and places are confused; words are entirely misunderstood, causing complete mistranslation; the caution which Orosius now and again expressed in making a statement is here neglected; and matters noted as doubtful or possible by him are stated simply by Alfred as true. Much, moreover, of the Latin work is here omitted, especially material relating to the times of the Caesars; and the seven books of the original are represented in the Anglo-Saxon by six. Alfred was fortunate, of course, in having a Christian authority in Orosius for all this pagan matter. Even so, he adds here and there a purely Christian touch on his own. He makes the pagan Leonidas place his trust "in God" and declares that Hannibal "said within himself that he was longing and hoping for dominion over Rome, but that God would not allow it."

In spite, however, of all the king's strenuous endeavor, many men of Wessex in this ninth century must have found their minds sinking and slipping as in a bog of clay when they strove to read this Anglo-Saxon version of Orosius. One hopes that their eyes lighted up when they fell on a few pages near the beginning of the book, amid Alfred's translation of a discourse on world geography which Orosius had placed before his long treatment of history. For here the king, most happily for all his readers, medieval and modern, decided to insert a substantial addition of his own in regard to the Germany and the Scandinavia of this ninth century, those countries so well known by name in his England and among his own people.

His description of Germany's geography is of deep interest to scholars, since it shows the knowledge of that country current in Alfred's time. But the famous picture of the northern lands of Europe is even more fascinating. And here the king had firsthand evidence. He was drawing his words from two explorers who had traveled far in the north and had themselves, he said, told him of what they had seen.

The name, in Anglo-Saxon form, of one of these sailors was Ohthere, and he is here described as acknowledging Alfred, king of Wessex, as "his lord." Ohthere, however, was a Norwegian, and many have wondered what this statement means. As one observer has remarked, it can hardly have been due to gratitude for hospitality received by him in Wessex. Nor is there any evidence that Ohthere had met Alfred before he made his explorations in the north. He told the king that he lived farther north in Norway than any of his fellow-countrymen, on the coast of the "West Sea," by which he meant the Norwegian Sea, and that his "shire" of Norway was Helgeland.

In this region one enters the Arctic Circle. It is known to many for the islands which cluster about its shore, broken by long, narrow fjords, for its valleys and the great waterfalls that roar down their cliffs in its southerly part, and for that far-stretching glacier, the Svartisen, the field of "Black Ice." This land, Ohthere said, extended very far in length, but was very narrow in width. He could use for pasture or for plowing only that part of it which lay near the sea, and even that was very rocky here and there. Farther inland rose wild mountains, inhabited by Lapps (he called them "Finns"). North of him the land stretched on, holding only a few Lapps who lived by hunting in the winter and by fishing off the coast in summertime. In Helgeland, Ohthere told Alfred, there was such excellent whale-hunting that he and five other men had killed sixty whales in two days. Across the mountains from its more southerly part lay Sweden, and facing the more northerly part was a region which Alfred wrote down from Ohthere's report as "Cwenaland." This may have lain at the north end of the Gulf of Bothnia. Its people, the "Cwenas," now and then made raids across the mountains upon the men of Norway, carrying with them their boats, very small and very light, which they used in ferrying across the large fresh-water lakes among the mountains. These "Cwenas," it seems, were of Finnish race. Ohthere said that they in their turn were raided by the men of Helgeland, the "Northmen," as he called them.

He himself, he said, was one of the leading men of Helgeland and very wealthy in one of its sources of revenue, the wild reindeer, which he hunted and sold. At the time he came to Alfred he had six hundred of these deer in stock, tame and awaiting sale, as well as six most precious "decoy reindeer," which he used for capturing others of their kind. For all his standing, however, and his wealth of deer, he had no more than twenty head of horned cattle, twenty sheep, twenty pigs, and some horses with which he plowed a small tract of soil.

Another source of his income, as he reported it, is of interest. It consisted of tribute paid in kind, to him and to his neighbors in that northerly region, by the Lapps: furs and skins of reindeer, bear, marten, and otter; feathers of birds; ship's ropes made from hides of whale and seal. Tribute was exacted from these Lapps, he said, more or less in amount, according to the rank and importance of each one of them among his fellow-tribesmen.

This detail of Ohthere's story has brought forth an interesting suggestion which might explain his coming to Alfred. Historians of Norway are now inclined to date the great battle of Hafrsfjord, in which Harold Fairhair finally won dominion over its land, about the year 885. Even before this time Harold had been winning lordship and control; and there is evidence which at least points toward his seizing of the *finnskattr*, these taxes paid by the Lapps, as his own royal prerogative. It is known that many brave men sailed away from Norway in their anger against what they held as the usurpation of Harold Fairhair. Perhaps Ohthere was one of these; perhaps he sailed to Wessex to enter the service of another king, one by this time renowned for the defense of his own people against invasion.

Ohthere went on to tell of his voyages. He had been curious, he told Alfred, to find out how far land extended north of his own most northerly point and whether any people, except those few Lapps, lived in its solitudes. He had, therefore, started out in his boat from his home in Helgeland on a journey due north to explore. As Alfred's geography here is difficult to understand, and as the political geography of Europe has changed within recent years in regard to borderlands and the names of towns, it will be better perhaps to describe the explorations of these two sailors, Ohthere and Wulfstan, in modern terms.

Ohthere, then, took his boat northward past islands innumerable, past Hammerfest, past the North Cape, as far as the entrance to the Barents Sea. Then he voyaged southeast, waiting at times for a favorable wind, and quite uncertain of what he would find as he went on. Past Varangerfjord and onward he continued for four days. By their end he had reached the bend of the Kola Peninsula, and now he turned toward its southern border and the entrance to the White Sea. He sailed into the sea and continued in its waters for five days, along the southern coast of the peninsula, until he reached the mouth of a great river. During the whole of his course hitherto he had seen only Lapp hunters. But now he, and the man or two whom he had taken with him for his aid, saw that the land beyond this river's mouth was inhabited, and they were afraid of encountering some enemy tribe if they continued on their course as before.

This river was probably the Varzuga, which flows down through the southern part of the Kola Peninsula into the White Sea. Ohthere, wisely cautious, turned his boat up the river and there found more cultivated land. Again fearing attack, he did not dare to put his boat into shore. But soon he came upon men who dwelt along the Kandalaksha Gulf, probably in what is now Karelo-Finnish territory; in Alfred's narrative these men are called "Beormas." They must have been friendly, for, Ohthere said, they told him "many tales." He had already heard of their people in his own country; for the Norwegians, who thought of them as dwellers in "Bjarmaland," believed this to be a faraway region of magic, of a people who confounded their enemies by mysterious incantations which caused the heavens suddenly to burst open at time of battle and hurl down fearful deluges of rain and hail. The "Beormas" told Ohthere about Lapp neighbors of theirs who, it would seem, spoke almost the same language as themselves. Alfred wrote of these neighbors as the "Terfinnas"; and we may think of them as living along the south shore of the White Sea. Ohthere's chief interest in visiting this region was its walrus-hunting, and he brought some walrus tusks as a gift to the king.

There were other voyages, too, of which Ohthere told Alfred. He had sailed not only north from Helgeland but also south, past Iceland in the distance, although, as several scholars have noted, he did not mention it; along the

Norwegian Sea into the North Sea and round into the Skagerrak, until he reached the coast of Vestfold in southern Norway. And then again he had sailed on from there, skirting the west coast of Sweden for three days, along the Kattegat into the Store, or the Great Belt, past the Danish islands of Fyn and Sjælland, of Langeland and Lolland, to the port of Hedeby, near Slesvig.

The other voyager, Wulfstan, the second source of Alfred's additions to Orosius, was apparently an Englishman. He had taken his boat from Hedeby, then a Danish port, past Lolland and Bornholm into the Baltic Sea, to reach the country about the mouth of the Wista and the Gulf of Danzig. Here, he told Alfred, he had met the people who lived near the Zalew Wislany, the salt-water inlet which lies between Gdansk in Poland and Kaliningrad in the Soviet Union. Wulfstan went on to describe their manner of living. They possessed many towns, he said, each one ruled by a king. They lived largely on fish and honey; mares' milk was the drink of the dominant minority who were steppe folk, and mead was left for the poor and the slaves. No ale was brewed among them.

But, especially, the customs attending death among this people seem to have impressed Wulfstan. He reported to Alfred that the body of the dead lay in state among his kinsmen and friends for a month, or two months, sometimes even for six. The higher the rank of the dead, the longer it lay. All this time, around the bier in the house, there was carousal of drinking and celebration of funeral games. At last came the day decided upon for the burning of the body. Then the dead man's treasures, those which could be carried, were divided into five or six or even more shares, according to their number and value. The richest portion was laid on the ground about a mile from the dead man's home, and all the other portions at points between the first one and the home, each one nearer than the last, the portion of least value being placed nearest the house. After this had been carefully done, all the men who owned the swiftest horses rode from a point five or six miles distant in a race to pick up these treasures, and the prizes fell to those who reached them first. Finally, the cremation of the dead man, clothed in his best and girded with his weapons, was solemnly fulfilled.

Swift horses, as we may imagine, sold for a high price in that country. If anyone asks how its dead could remain so long within their homes, the answer of Wulfstan is that certain men dwelling there possessed the secret of refrigeration; even in summertime, he said, they could keep water frozen into ice.

To all these tales of Ohthere and Wulfstan, Alfred had surely listened with rapt mind. Books, we know, were worth the world to him; yet in reality his world was the people of his land. To pass on to them, not only books, but the narratives of those who themselves had heard and seen strange things, and heard and seen, too, things that concerned the Europe of Alfred's own day, narratives that told of the Northmen from whom had descended so much tribulation upon England and who were even now settled on wide regions of English land—this to the king of Wessex was welcome and happy work, good both for himself and for those whom he longed to teach.

2

From facts and details of history Alfred now went on to the more difficult matter of thought and its discussion, into the sureties, and the questions, too, of philosophy and of religion. Here was increasing joy for him, in the turning of his mind to the high realities of his faith, in the more strenuous endeavor to bring these realities home to other men through words of their native speech. This time his choice of a Latin original for translation fell upon the book of a writer of the sixth century, the 500's after Christ, a writer and a book very different from Orosius and his *Histories*.

Yet again Alfred's choice was a natural one. The writer was Boethius, a leading minister of state and senate in the government of Rome under a barbarian king, Theodoric the Goth, ruler of Italy from 493 until 526; for by this time the Roman Empire in the West had fallen before the barbarian advance. In 476 Odoacer had driven from Italy's throne its last Roman possessor; in 493 Theodoric had marched with his Goths to wrest in his turn this throne from Odoacer, even, so men declared, to kill his fellow-barbarian with his own hand.

King Theodoric and his Gothic warriors, who now held and defended Italy against other barbarian attack, were not heathen. Their fathers had been taught to revere the name of Christ, but a Christ essentially removed from the *Deum verum de Deo vero; Genitum non factum, consubstantialem Patri* of the Catholic church. In other words, Theodoric the king was an Arian heretic to that church which his Roman subjects revered.

Boethius, though a member of one of the most aristo-

cratic and distinguished families of Rome, yet for that
Rome's sake held office in its government under this barbarian conqueror of his land. The story of his fall from
office and of his imprisonment and execution under Theodoric is well known. He was charged with treason
against the king, a charge still unproved. If he was guilty,
he was guilty for the service, he believed, of the Rome
and the Italy he loved so well. It may be that he died a
victim to the fears of his less courageous associates in the
politics of Rome.

In the nine months or so that he spent in prison, day
by day uncertain of his final fate, which came upon him,
with torture, it was said, in 524, he wrote that famous
book, *The Consolation of Philosophy,* which, repeatedly
read and translated into many tongues, has borne its influence and its tradition down the centuries of time. It
is the story of a man's struggle with his rebellion against
the pain which has come upon him, pain which he holds
undeserved and, therefore, evil. Boethius cast his story in
the form of a dialogue, of alternating Latin prose and
verse. To him, he writes, miserable and angry in his cell,
suddenly appeared the Lady Philosophy, his patron, counselor and friend of happier days, to reproach and rebuke
him for his wandering from her citadel, the home of the
One and Only Good, and for his forgetfulness of the
nature and the source of true happiness.

First, then, in this dialogue Philosophy allows Boethius
to pour forth all his passion of complaint. Then slowly
she begins to hold out before his wounded and darkened
soul that light of sound doctrine which is to draw him
back from the quicksands of unreality once more to safe

lodging upon her rock of Truth. The argument passes from the unmasking of fickle Fortune, now kind, now adverse; from the revealing of the sure and lasting content known only to the soul that rests upon the One Unity, the One Good, and, therefore, the One Joy, which all men desire and which all men are seeking in their many, often foolish ways; to the thought of Providence, of Free Will, of Fate, and of the problems these present; and, finally, to the vision of the One Supreme Good, ever beholding from His eternal life of utter tranquillity the tossing waves of human time, past, present, and to be; ever knowing what has been, is, and will be for each man, yet never compelling it; ever desiring each man's happiness and peace in and through Himself.

Here scholars of modern times begin their chorus of criticism. Nothing, they declare, in this *Consolation of Philosophy* proves that Boethius was a Catholic Christian. His argument, they say, is largely drawn from Platonic and Neo-Platonic teachings. True, answer other scholars, yet nothing written here proves that Boethius was *not* a Christian. A man may hold his religion without plainly declaring it in his written work; and there are various reasons why Boethius may have chosen to write in Platonic rather than in Catholic words this encouragement of his, sent forth from his prison to other men, pagan or Christian, in like bitterness of soul.

When, however, we come to Alfred and his version of this book, we find no doubts at all. To him the "One Supreme Goodness and Unity" of Boethius meant simply the God of the Christian faith, and the more so since he had read other men of the Middle Ages who held the same view. At the beginning of his work the king placed an introductory chapter, based on one of those medieval "Lives" of Boethius which described the Roman philosopher as a martyr to his soul's loyalty. In this chapter, then, Alfred shows us this martyr, held fast in prison for his courage, for his upholding of the Catholic church against her Arian enemy, Theodoric the king. Later on, more than once Alfred himself bursts out against Theodoric in angry words.

The thought and the discussion in this book of Boethius, so far as King Alfred understood it, were of intense interest to him, first for its own sake and nature, then for its lesson to men in general. At the same time it must be remembered that Alfred was not skilled in the terms and the reasoning of classical philosophy; that the argument of Boethius here often eluded his grasp; that, moreover, the Latin itself of Boethius, formal and elaborate in its brilliance, offered to this English king difficulty at times insuperable.

Alfred, however, was eager, as before, to draw from these riches consolation and instruction for his own people, far removed from the learning of the Roman Boethius. He decided, therefore, in following the lines and the guidance of his original, to set himself here very largely free from adherence to its letter; to draw from it what he would and could; to add and change as he would. The result was really a book of his own, stamped from beginning to end with his own character, inspired by his faith: a vivid, warm, clear, and simple discourse on the Christian God as the Center and Foundation, the Life Eternal of all souls in this world and beyond.

Men were grateful to Alfred for his decision. Ethelweard, known as "the Chronicler," who late in the tenth century made a Latin rendering of one version of the *Anglo-Saxon Chronicle*, wrote that in this Anglo-Saxon book of the king "not only for its more cultured readers, but even for those who heard it read aloud, the mournful book of Boethius seemed to quicken with fresh life." Here, certainly, Alfred owed much to men who had worked before him. That historian of the twelfth century, William of Malmesbury, tells us that, before Alfred began his version, his teacher, Asser, "worked out for him the meaning of this book of Boethius in words easier to understand, a labor necessary in those days, though it would be absurd in ours; but so the King requested, that he might more easily translate it into English." It is often unwise to trust William of Malmesbury's statements too far; yet this one may well be based on truth. We do not know how much, also, of the writing in Alfred's book that is not found in Boethius was due, in word or by suggestion, to this counselor of his.

Nor do we know, and this is even a more interesting question, how much Alfred drew from written Christian commentaries on this famous Latin *Consolation of Philosophy*. We know that he used the work of Remigius of Auxerre, that ninth-century pupil of Irish tradition who lectured at Paris, and at Reims when Fulk was archbishop, and who thought it his duty to bring out clearly the Christian character which he believed to lie imbedded under the Platonic surface of this book. Some of Alfred's definitely Catholic discussion here was taken from Remigius, as research has shown; probably more was taken from other, similar sources.

We come, then, to Alfred's work, to look briefly at

what in it is entirely his own, or was made his own, as he absorbed it from the thought of Boethius and the teaching of these medieval Christian commentators. To him, above all, the Way of Consolation is God himself: *Se Weg is God.* Along this Way man travels, by God and in God, to God himself, who is for man his path and his arriving and his journey's end, both his road of learning and his attaining to knowledge. Not with pride may man travel along this road, but through the Valley of Humility and in the remembrance of that Wisdom which he desires; for in the Valley's depths he shall find Christ, his Lord. Neither the wind of strong afflictions nor the rain of heavy anxiety must turn him from his going. Should riches of this world come to him on the way, he will never forget that these in themselves are good, as the gift of God, and only become evil through man himself, when he covets them or misuses them as the devil wills, when he looks to them for that soul's content which he may find only in their Creator and his. The high standing of evil men will not distress him; for often this standing falls in ruin, as a tree falls suddenly with a loud crash in the forest when one least expects it. The lamps along this road to eternity—faith and holy love and hope—will shine out to guide him as he travels on, and woe will be his if in his haste and bustle he take his eyes away from their light, for then he will run in the strange darkness of this world's cares.

Nor is there always dull plodding on from day to day. Now and then Wisdom lifts her servants up above this stormy world into the still air of contemplation, even as the eagle soars into peace above the clouds that lower on the earth. Then shall the vision come to him: of God whom all things serve, whether they know it or know it not; who holds all things with the bridle of his hand and suffers them not to stray further than the length of his rein; who bids things contrary to one another, fire and water, earth and sea, winter and summer, life and death, so to contend that in the reality of his sight they sustain and support each other by the power of his will.

All, therefore, writes Alfred, is of God, the greater and the less: the sun and the little stars which twinkle in the night; the tiny brook which runs to meet the river and the river winding toward the sea; all come from him and find in him once more their home. As the wall of every house is fastened securely both upon the floor and in the roof, so God is both floor and roof for the soul of every man. As a wheel turns on its axle, and around the axle in the hub are fastened the spokes, and the spokes run between the axle and the wheel's rim; so God, the center and axle, carries and controls the wagon of humanity, bearing nearest him the hub of his saints, and in the spokes those middle men who live their lives between him, the axle, and the world, the wheel's rim, yet are themselves, nevertheless, of the body of his church and charge. As the wheel turns, now up, now down, on its course, so does the human spirit. "When it thinketh upon its Creator, then it is above itself; and when on itself, then it is within itself; and it is under itself when it loves the things of earth and makes much of them." The end of the wagon's journey is that heavenly Jerusalem where man's spirit shall need no longer the lamps of its long, dark road, but where it shall forever behold in new vision the finished fulfilment of God's desire.

By such simple words and illustrations of everyday life

Alfred tried to pass on to his men of Wessex the philosophy of consolation which the learned had long known in Boethius. Sometimes even more spontaneous workings of the king's mind meet us as we read, breaking through the form of his original: the pole stars of the Wain, the Wagon, turning on their path through the night; the white caps of the rising sea, warning the wise sailor to lower his mast and furl his sail; hunting dogs running along the hills and through the woods. Much is added in this Anglo-Saxon version to explain geography, history, mythology; and sometimes this, too, reflects the translator's thought. From medieval Latin comment Alfred borrowed also that touch of allegory which saw in the fall of Orpheus, looking back to his beloved, the evil fate of the sinner who, after turning in penitence toward the light of heaven, looks back again to his old sins and loses all he had hoped to gain. Classical story shows fresh color when Alfred with a sigh pictures its Golden Age of Peace and Plenty as a far-off time in which "no one had yet heard of Viking ships of war."

Much, also, that concerns the practical comes into view here from his thought. In everything, to this busy king, there must be planning and order; "for all that one begins at the wrong time has no good ending." There must be tools and material ready to each man's hand for his work; and here we come upon Alfred's well-known picture of a king's necessities. A king, he writes, must have abundance of men for his service: men to pray, and men to fight, men to labor with their hands, men to hold his trust as his friends. For the sustaining in goodly discipline of these men, the king's "tools," he must have material in plenty: gifts and weapons and food and ale and clothes. But all, tools and material, must be ruled and overseen by Wisdom, in a service which is not serfdom but liberty. And so Alfred ends his picture with his own desire: "I have longed to live worthily all my life, and thus to leave to those who shall come after me my memory in good works."

All this rendering was made in English prose, including the songs placed by Boethius on the lips of Philosophy, songs in various meters, some part of which Alfred omitted toward the end of his translating. There is another, a second, rendering of these songs in alliterative metrical Anglo-Saxon lines, made from Alfred's prose. Around this second rendering much controversy has swirled, debating whether this, too, was made by the king, or whether some other man made it, perhaps at Alfred's request. Its weakness of composition, experts have argued, makes it inferior to Alfred's own prose version. Why should he have made so poor a metrical translation after he had made so decent a showing in prose? Against this, others have retorted that Alfred loved Anglo-Saxon verse. Why should he not have tried his hand at this, even if the result to critics was less than admirable? In a preface, found at the beginning of the prose rendering, it is declared that the king did make from his prose translation a second, a metrical, version of the songs. Here, of course, it has been questioned whether Alfred wrote this preface. Recent thought, however, has inclined toward him as author of both renderings, in meter as in prose. After all, another attempt at verse has been granted him, that one in the second Preface to his

Pastoral Care, verse composed in metrical lines declaring the praise of St. Gregory of Rome, as well as in the ending of that same book, in the hymn to the Holy Spirit, Lord and Giver of learning.

3

From Platonic original, unilluminated by definite Christian doctrine, Alfred turned to medieval Latin philosophy, Platonic and Neo-Platonic, brought forward in the service of the Catholic faith. This he found in one of the earlier writings of that same Augustine of Hippo whom he had known through the work of Orosius.

At the time of this writing Augustine was not at Hippo; indeed, he was far from his future destiny as bishop and saint. He was only in his thirty-third year, although already he had known what other men would know, if at all, after a lifetime of experience. He had learned all that Carthage in Africa, his native country, could teach him; he had loved a woman who bore him a son outside of wedlock; by his wayward and un-Christian youth he had nearly broken his mother's heart; he had slipped away from his home to take passage for Italy, to teach in Rome, and to win a chair of rhetoric in Milan; he had wandered through the fascinating lowlands and highlands of Manichaeism and Neo-Platonism and had found no rest for his soul; and at last, in the garden at Milan, like St. Paul upon the Damascus road, he had met face to face the light of Catholic reality.

It was to him as a star seen in the East, and from that moment he had abandoned all to follow it in his search for further truth. Long and hard work on his lectures, together with his own inner questionings, had made rest imperative, and he now went with a few young men, close friends of his and of the same philosophic and inquiring mind, to a country house amid the mountains north of Milan. There, we are told, he spent his days in prayer, in writing letters, in discussion with these friends, and many hours of the night alone, wrestling with the problems of his own mind.

The substance of his thinking in these hours Augustine put together in two books which he called *Soliloquies*, written as a dialogue of debate between himself, the seeker, and his own faculty of Reason, now and throughout his later years the servant and aid of his faith. In this brief dialogue, which he left unfinished, he gives us, it is true, little of the breadth and depth of vision of his *Confessions*, published when his thought was far more mature. Much of the *Soliloquies* is matter of dialectical argument, of absorbing subject but in manner rather dull and dry, a manner reminiscent, perhaps, of his chair of rhetoric in Milan. We find our interest here, and it is very real, in seeing him in the ecstasy of a decision made, a struggle past, in the faith, lately attained, that now for him God is: in his earth, in his children, in the secret ways of knowledge; above all and in all, in the Catholic church, in her sacraments and in her mystic power of prayer.

Guided and supported by prayer, he began his *Soliloquies* and carried the work forward in this retreat of leisure during the winter of 386–87, while he was making ready for his baptism, given him in 387, by St. Ambrose, then bishop of Milan, doubtless on Holy Saturday, the eve of Easter. The keynote is struck at once. "What do you desire to know?" asks his Reason.

"I want to know God and the soul."

"Nothing more?"

"Nothing at all." Bidden by Reason, he enters upon his search. It leads him to declare that the soul, by the aid of faith, hope, and charity, must first strive to gain for herself sound health, which will enable her to search and, in searching, to see. Toward Wisdom she will direct her eyes; and all that a man possesses, riches or friendship or marriage or honors or life itself, may only be held by him as a means of furthering the quest of his soul.

Since, then, life is the search for truth, the thought of death is intolerable if it means the death, not only of the body, but of the soul. For the death of the soul means that its progress toward Wisdom, toward God, must cease, that all hope of attaining its desire will be at an end. Here, then, Reason leads her pupil into an argument for the eternal living of the soul. What is true, she declares, can never die; Truth holds her home in the soul; therefore, as truth is eternal, so death can never destroy her necessary and inevitable dwelling place, the soul of man.

The dialogue breaks off, leaving Augustine still afraid that death brings to man oblivion, even of all that he has learned of God in his earthly pilgrimage. Later on, of course, he wrote much on the soul's eternal destiny. And, too, in the last years of his life, as he reconsidered his various writings, he found fault with this one for its Neo-Platonic thought. He had been wrong, he said, in believing that the soul must flee from the joys of sense lest "with their sticky matter" they hinder her wings from bearing her upward from the dark cave of her earthly prison to her native air on high. By this time Augustine had long known that the Lord who himself was made flesh had willed all things to be good and wonderful. He found fault here, also, with his leaning in these early *Soliloquies* toward the Platonic doctrine that souls, pent within the body, forget what once they knew before their descent to this earth, that by strong effort of discipline they must recall lost truth. No, said Augustine in this reconsidering, man's knowledge comes from that illuminating which is from God alone.

But it was not for dialectical argument that Alfred put his mind to labor on the *Soliloquies*. It was because he found here once again the teaching of Boethius that the Way is God. The words which Augustine wrote at the beginning of his work sent Alfred back once more across the centuries for inspiration in his own and his country's need:

Thou art One God, one eternal and true Substance; in Whom is no discrepancy, no confusion, no passing, no lack, no death; with Whom is fullness of harmony, of certainty, of content, of life. Thou art He Whom all things obey; by Whose laws the poles turn, the stars abide by their paths, the sun drives the day, the moon holds in curb the night; by Whose laws the months wax and wane, the years follow their seasons; through Whose laws the changing order of things is held constant in the rein of circling times; through Whose laws the soul is free to meet its joy or its misery, its punishing or its reward: God, from Whom come to us all things of good, by Whom are held from us all things of evil; God, above Whom, beyond Whom, without Whom, there is nought; God, beneath Whom, in Whom, with Whom, is all.

King Alfred called his version of these *Soliloquies* his "Flowers." He added to the material which he gathered from this work of Augustine passages culled from a number of other writings, especially others by this same saint of Hippo. He omitted a great deal of Augustine's dialectical reasoning, was content to rest upon the authority of the Bible and the Fathers of the church, and added much, too, which was drawn from his own thought, both as a king and as a simple man.

He starts from the same point as his guide, Augustine, with the search for knowledge of God and the soul. As he goes on, he tries, as before, to illustrate and to explain by pictures of his own from ordinary human life. Here is one:

Therefore it is needful that thou look straight with the eyes of thy spirit to God, as straight as a cable stretches taut from a ship to her anchor. Then, as the anchor is fixed firmly in the earth, so do thou fasten thine eyes to God. Even though the ship tosses at sea in the waves, yet she is safe and unbroken as long as her cable holds fast to her anchor. And with these anchors—wisdom and humility and prudence and moderation and justice and mercy and reason and maturity of mind and goodwill and cleanness and abstinence—with these thou shalt fasten firmly to God the cable that shall keep safe the ship of thy soul.

Here is another illustration which every man could understand:

He who would see Wisdom with the eyes of his soul must climb upward, little by little, as a man climbing some cliff on the seashore by a ladder, step by step. When, if ever, he is high upon the cliff, then he can look out upon the view over shore and sea, now lying before his gaze.

Again and again illustration is made here from the life of a king amid his people. As men travel their different roads toward the royal court, Alfred writes, and some find the road long and hard and muddy while others find it short and easy and well paved, so it is with those bound for the House of Wisdom. And even within that house, when pilgrims have found their way to it, some are lodged in comfort and dignity, others in humble places, others even in prison. Yet, just as all visitors to the king's court, however different the quarters allotted them, receive sustenance and protection from one and the same lord, so Wisdom gives of her light to every man, according to her will and to his power to see.

At the end of the second book of these "Flowers," which in the Latin *Soliloquies* left Augustine still unsatisfied, Alfred, also, tells Reason that he is still afraid. May it not be, he asks, that man's understanding in the world beyond this life shall remain only that of a mere child? Will man's soul really live to grow up? Reason encourages yet further search; and Alfred adds a third book, in which he seeks, from his readings in various Fathers and from his own thought, to describe in some part the life of those departed hence.

All souls, he writes here, the good and the bad, who have departed this life know what is happening, both on earth and, also, in the world in which they now are, though they will not know everything until the Day of Judgment. All, too, have very constant remembrance of their kinsfolk and friends on earth.

The good souls in the world beyond help the good

still on earth in every way they can. But they have no desire to aid the wicked they knew on earth, because these themselves have no wish to forsake their evil ways. These good souls in the life beyond are entirely free and are the beloved of the king; they look from their own joy upon the torments of the wicked for the increasing of their own sense of the divine mercy. Often do they call to mind the various seasons, of happiness and of sorrow, of their life on earth; and they rejoice exceedingly that neither in easy days nor in hard and bitter ones did they forsake the will of their Lord.

The wicked, too, see God, like guilty men condemned before some king on earth. But to them the sight of God, the sight of his saints in ecstasy of fulfilled desire, adds torment to their punishing. Yet all in hell do not suffer equally, even as all in heaven do not have equal glory. Each soul, in heaven or in hell, will be given his due according to his earning on earth. "The like have their like" in the life of the world to come. Nor will all in heaven be possessed of equal wisdom; this, also, will depend on each man's use of his time in this world. The more a man toils here, the more he longs for holy wisdom, the more shall be his in the hereafter. Yet all, according to God's promise, shall receive of wisdom to their hearts' desire, each according to his power to receive; and all in far greater measure than the uttermost of ancient days, the high-water mark of earth-bound minds.

"Nothing will He conceal from us Who gives it to us to know Himself. Then shall we know all that now we want to know, and that, too, which now we do not want to know. Then shall we all, the worst and the best of us, meet the Vision of God, then shall we all at last know, for our torment or for our content."

4

We come, now, to the end of Alfred's books, of his efforts to translate and to explain to his people of Wessex the history and geography of England and of the world, the truths and the problems of philosophy and of religion. When he had begun this long labor, he had written an explanation, placed at the beginning of his *Pastoral Care*, of the reason for his undertaking and of the manner in which he was trying to carry out the work. Now, as his labor drew to its close, he wanted to tell his people, the intellectual and the simple, just what he had tried to do, the joy which his work had given him, the hope which was in him that other translators would follow in his steps.

He placed, therefore, another preface at the beginning of these "Flowers" collected in this, the last book made for the educating of his land. This preface was written in the same homely language which had marked so much of his work, and, as before, it took its thought from the everyday life of Wessex. In it we find two parables. The first describes the king driving his wagon, the wagon of his mind and spirit, again and again to the forest of knowledge, loading it there with all the twigs and timbers, that is, with all the facts and thoughts it can bear, and joyously carrying home his burden. Once at home, again and again he has set to work to build houses, by which in his parable he means books of instruction and of counsel, from these collected twigs and timbers, these facts and thoughts gathered by him in his reading, for his own happiness and for the comfort and welfare of his subjects. May many other men, he hopes, also make their way to the same forest and bring back the same timbers for the building of many other houses of wisdom, spiritual and secular, in the days to come.

The work, he tells us, has been hard and difficult. Now, perhaps, since his wars are over, his laws made, and his books written, God of his goodness may give to the days left to him of this present life a greater measure of ease and comfort. For, though his work for his people is nearly ended, his course on earth is not yet fully run.

Here we come to the second parable. On this earth, like other men, he has lived in happiness through the gift of God. Pleasures have been his, work has been his, through the power of him who creates all. Yet these pleasures, this work, endure only for a season; all has been temporary, destined sooner or later to end. And yet not to end; rather, to find its fulfilment. It is for him, as it is for every man, so to live and work on earth that from the house which he has built here, from the work which by God's will he has loved in this fleeting life, he may pass with sure and certain hope on to the eternal dwelling, to the work which has no end, to that far more joyous life, that infinite increasing of knowledge in the nearer Presence of God.

Here is this last preface which Alfred wrote, translated into modern words:

I gathered for myself stout poles and upright beams and crossbeams, and handles for all the tools with which I could work, and pieces of wood for bolts and for slanting supports, to use in every work which I could fulfil, the most beautiful timbers, and as many as I could carry away. And I did not come home with just one single burden, nor did I want to bring home the whole forest, even if I could have carried it away. In every tree I saw something which I needed at home.

So I counsel everyone who is strong and has many wagons to make his way to that same forest where I cut those upright beams, there to get him more of these timbers, and to load his wagons, too, with fair twigs; that from all these he may weave many a fine wall, and raise many a beautiful house, and make a goodly estate, fenced within its own land, and there live pleasantly and peacefully, winter and summer, as I so far have not done.

He who taught me, who have loved the forest, He can give it me to live more pleasantly, both in this transitory dwelling by the wayside, while I am in this world, and also in the eternal home which He has promised us through Saint Augustine and Saint Gregory and Saint Jerome, and many other holy Fathers. I believe, also, that for their merits He will make this way for me better than it has been before; that, especially, He will so enlighten the eyes of my understanding that I may find the right road to the eternal home, to the eternal glory and the eternal rest, promised to us through the holy Fathers. So be it.

It is no wonder that a man likes to work on timber, both in the carrying forth and in the building. Every man, after he has built a cottage on lease from his lord and with his lord's help, wants to stay in it for a while, to hunt, to go fowling and fishing, and in every way to make use of it as his lease allows, both on sea and on land, until of his lord's kindness he comes to earn a freehold in perpetual right of ownership.

So may He do who gives richly, who rules not only these cottages, here granted on lease, but also those eternal dwellings. He who created both and rules both, may He grant that I fail not in either, but give it me to fulfil my service here and, above all, to reach that home beyond.

As one looks back upon the Anglo-Saxon Alfred in his writings, it is impossible to forget that he was born and brought up, that he lived and wrote, in a Wessex which gave to him fully of its Celtic heritage. Inextricably mingled with the Anglo-Saxon traditions of his kindred were a Celtic consciousness of Nature, a love of solitude, a passion for learning, a spirit of sacrifice which called him from youth until his death to give all that was in him, for his people, his country, and his God. These things, of course, were not peculiar to the Celt; but they rise from all Celtic life and literature to meet us with an intensity all their own. The learning of Wessex had been fostered under Aldhelm, in a monastery of Irish tradition; Alfred himself was taught day by day by a teacher he had called from Wales. These things surely had marked with their impress both the king himself and his work.

CHAPTER TEN

King Alfred AT HOME

IT IS SURPRISING that Asser, who wrote in such detail concerning King Alfred, tells us so little about his wife, the Mercian Lady Ealhswith. He praises Alfred's mother, Osburh, as "very devout, noble both in character and in race," and his mother-in-law, Eadburh, as a woman held in high respect; but he does not accord to Alfred's queen so much as her name. She survived her husband by some three years and after his death completed the work of monastic building in Winchester by founding a house of religion for nuns, known as the Nunnaminster, or as St. Mary's Abbey.

We are, indeed, led to believe that it was their father, the king, who influenced and guided the early years of the five surviving children whom Ealhswith bore to him. In this he did a notable work. The eldest, Ethelflaed, was given in marriage to Alfred's devoted friend, Ethelred, that ealdorman of Mercia who guarded and ruled London for his king. When Ethelflaed's husband died, twelve years after Alfred, she took the rule of Mercia into her own hands and worked strenuously with her brother Edward, now king of Wessex, to build fortresses for its defense. She died in 918, shortly after she had won from the Danes the borough towns of Derby and Leicester, with promise of their allegiance, and a like declaration of adherence from the people of York. History knows her as the "Lady of the Mercians."

Her brother, Alfred's second child, carried on his father's work splendidly as King Edward "the Elder." At his death in 924 Scandinavian England was once again under English rule as far north as the Humber. Then high courage and wisdom enabled Edward's son, that Athelstan whom Alfred, his grandfather, had invested with knightly cloak and sword in the hope of his promise, not only to bring the rulers of the north of England and of Wales beneath his influence as supreme lord but also greatly to confirm England's standing by powerful alliances with rulers on the Continent.

Alfred himself had made one of these alliances when he gave another daughter, Aelfthryth, as wife to Baldwin, count of Flanders. For many years the friendship thus confirmed between England and Flanders remained unbroken, a friendship of material importance to English politics. This Baldwin, we may note, was the son of the hotly contested marriage of Judith, Alfred's stepmother, with the young Baldwin "Iron-Arm," who had rescued her from her imprisonment in the castle of Senlis.

Several children of Alfred and Ealhswith, we are told,

died in infancy. Of the remaining two, one, Ethelgifu, became a nun and eventually abbess of a convent built by Alfred on the cliff at Shaftesbury in Dorsetshire. The early years of the youngest child, Ethelweard, must have given his father lively hope, for the boy had delighted him by his devotion to books. He and his sister Aelfthryth are especially named as receiving great care of instruction at home; and Ethelweard was one of the many boys educated at court in its "school" under the immediate direction of the king.

Sons of nobles and of simple men alike were taught in this "school" to read and to write both Latin and Anglo-Saxon, to learn by heart psalms and poems from Old English books. Discipline was strict, particularly for those who, as Alfred well knew, were destined in later days for places of high responsibility in their land. He also knew, however, how at times to relax this discipline. He tempered his strictness by leading out his young wards, those soldiers, bishops, and diplomats of the future, to hunt in the forest, to enjoy that diversion so dear to himself; and now and then he went off to train with equal enthusiasm the men who kept his royal falcons and hawks and hounds ready for these hours of hunting. Battles and books, diplomacy and sport, were all properly a part of the life of kings and men of high degree in King Alfred's England.

It was through his devotion to his country, doubtless, and his interest in its history that Alfred turned his mind to those Old English annals known as the *Anglo-Saxon Chronicle*. All scholars agree that they were compiled during his reign; but experts differ in their theories regarding the manner and the source of this compiling. It has been variously argued that the work up to and including Alfred's reign to the year 891 was done in his time; again, that the compilers possessed for their use a set of earlier annals and that they continued these to include Alfred's reign; again, that the work was done under Alfred, probably at Winchester; and, yet again, on the other hand, that the work was carried out, not directly under Alfred, but under one of his nobles as patron, and very possibly near the boundary of Somerset and Dorset, in southwestern England.

At all events, the compiling must have been watched with intense interest by this king. It was to be of untold value. Asser, for instance, used these annals constantly in his *Life* of Alfred.

2

As we have seen, Alfred's enthusiasm for men who could aid him and bring him knowledge was not bounded by England. We have followed his connections with Welshmen, with Franks, with Italians, with Norwegians. His *Life* tells, too, of welcome given by him to men of Brittany and of Frisia in the Netherlands. The visitors were not only men whom he had invited or looked forward to receiving. Against the year 891 the Old English annals relate that three Irishmen came from Ireland in a boat which had no oars and which was made of hides. Their journey took them a week. Then, just as their store of food was running out, they landed on the Cornish coast and before long made their way to King Alfred. He received them gladly when they said to him that they had "stolen away because they wanted for love of God to be on pilgrimage, they cared not where." Their names were Dubslane, Macbeth, and Maelinmun.

To Rome, Alfred continued the devotion of his father, Ethelwulf. Under him alms were sent repeatedly there from "the West Saxons and King Alfred"; entries in the *Chronicle* mention such dispatches against the years 883, 887, 888, and 890. Marinus, who was pope from 882 until his death in 884, freed that English quarter in Rome, the "Schola Saxonum," from payment of taxes at Alfred's asking. Gifts of high value were also sent by this pope to Alfred, one "a fragment of the Cross of Christ." We have seen, too, that the king received letters, gifts, and prescriptions for remedies in sickness from Elias the Third, Patriarch of Jerusalem. Another story, recorded of the year 883 by manuscripts of the *Chronicle* which date long after Alfred's time, and also found in William of Malmesbury, that historian of the twelfth century, declares that Alfred sent alms to India in honor of St. Thomas and St. Bartholomew, the Apostles, held in tradition as missionaries to that country. Whether this detail is true or not, and just what may be meant here by "India," we cannot tell.

3

Behind and beneath all those daily labors and secular duties of Alfred which we have followed in this book lay always his devotion to his faith, not only in word and in offering, but in practice. Every morning he was in his place at Mass; regularly he observed the Hours of the church; often he was found at night in his chapel, absorbed in solitary prayer, reciting psalms from his "Handbook." William of Malmesbury, indeed, tells us that Alfred began to translate the Psalter from Latin into Anglo-Saxon but died when he had hardly finished the first part. Much discussion has centered around the question whether we still have this translation of his, if he did make it, in the prose portion of the manuscript known as the *Paris Psalter* (Paris, Bibl. Nat. lat. 8824, fol 1*a*–63*b*). Evidence of similarity in wording and in style between this and the Anglo-Saxon versions of the Boethius and the *Pastoral Care* of St. Gregory, both attributed to Alfred, make the theory, if not proved, at least possible and surely attractive.

Like many of us, in our resolutions for Lent or for the New Year, Alfred, it would seem, drew up elaborate schemes in an endeavor to spend his money and his time as his conscience bade him. At any rate, Asser, who was his constant companion and confidant, reports that the king solemnly resolved to devote half his available income and half his working hours to the direct service of God and that he did his best to carry out his vow. There is no reason to reject this statement. Of course, in the midst of continual interruptions and obligations, the king must very often have fallen short of what he held as his ideal. Yet a glance at this ideal will throw light on his character.

He planned, then, every year to divide the money at his disposal for distribution, revenues from royal estates and taxes and other sources, into two equal parts, half for secular, half for religious purposes and carefully to allot each of these parts. The half to be devoted to secular uses was again in his plan divided into three equal portions: the first was to be distributed every year among the soldiers of his army and the various ministers and officials of his court; the second was to fall to the architects and craftsmen whom he had gathered from various countries for the restoring and ennobling of the structures on his lands; the third was to be given to strangers and pilgrims arriving in those lands, to each according to his need and to the necessities of his rank.

The second half, to be devoted to religious service, was apportioned into four parts. The first, Alfred decided, should be offered for the aid of the poor, of whatever country or nation, who came under his notice. Distribution of this charity, however, was to be made after due and proper investigation, according to the counsel of St. Gregory the Great: "Do not give little where much is needed, or much where little is enough." The second part was to be laid aside for the support of those two houses of religion, at Athelney and at Shaftesbury, which Alfred himself had built and filled. Neither of these was monastic in a full sense. Alfred was busy in trying to raise the level of Christian living and teaching among his subjects, not in reviving among them that regular and ascetic discipline once, in the seventh and eighth centuries, vigorously followed by English monks and nuns. These houses, however, were to be monastic, he hoped, in the sense that they would be centers of prayer for the support of himself and of the fighting, laboring world outside their doors. The third part was earmarked for his "school" of boys, gathered from many homes to his court. The fourth division he decided to distribute among churches and communities of clergy in Wessex, in Mercia, in Cornwall, Wales, Northumbria, Ireland, Brittany, and France in general, so far as his means would allow.

Distribution of his time was even more complicated and difficult. Time had to be reckoned in hours; but at night the darkness and by day the frequent clouds and rains made measurement after the current manner of water clocks and sundials often impossible, at least in any regular and trustworthy pattern. Here, then, once again the creative instinct of this king came to his aid. He ordered candles to be made of wax, each twelve inches long and carefully calculated to last four hours. Six of these were placed, one after another, to burn before the relics of the saints during the twenty-four hours of night and day. The plan has been marked as an interesting advance, perhaps original with Alfred, upon the English medieval system derived from Greece and Rome. This system had divided each day into twelve divisions in accordance with the sun's light, of longer hours on summer days, of shorter on those of winter. Alfred seems here to have tried to make equal days and nights for his work and rest, both those of winter and those of summer.

Trouble, nevertheless, at once arose to disturb this equal measuring. Draughts of wind rushed in through doors and windows, through chinks and cracks, to fan the candle flames into irregular and overspeedy consuming. In this dilemma the king decided to inclose each candle in its turn within a lantern, made with foundation of wood and with sides of translucent horn, where, he hoped, it might last its full course unhurried. We cannot think that every candle did exactly meet this aim; but presumably some measure of reckoning was achieved. We do not know, either, how far this lantern of horn was actually Alfred's invention. It would seem that he added from his own devising a little door of horn in the lantern's side for the replacing of candles as they burned down. Asser tells us that a lantern of this kind went with the king wherever he journeyed, to measure his hours of prayer and his work in churches, in manors, even in the tent of his encamping during time of war.

However ideal and impossible of complete achievement these plans of Alfred may seem, at least they reveal in him a determination to order his time and his resources aright, to devote to his faith and its biddings the same skill, reason, and energy which he used in the secular business of his reign.

4

Asser's last recorded date in his story of King Alfred was 887; and internal evidence, as we have noted, places its writing in 893. Little is known of external events after peace with the Danes came about in 896. The last year of Alfred's life shows him in council at Chelsea, discussing with his son-in-law, Ethelred, and his archbishop, Pleg-mund, plans for the restoration of London. He died on the twenty-sixth of October, 899, when he was not far from his fiftieth birthday. The *History of Saint Cuthbert*, found in a manuscript of the twelfth century, tells among its stories that in his last hours the king "called to his side his son Edward, intrusted to his care gifts for Saint Cuthbert's honoring, two circlets for the arm and a golden censer, and earnestly bade him to love God and this Saint and to place in them his hope, as he himself ever had done and still most zealously was doing."

He was buried in the Old Minster at Winchester, where, its clergy soon declared, "in insane imaginings, that his ghost in human form was roaming amid its buildings night after night." By that same son, now King Edward, his relics and those of his queen, Ealhswith, were removed to that New Minster which, as Alfred had wished and planned, was raised shortly after his death by Edward under direction of the wise and devoted priest Grimbald. In the twelfth century they were once more transferred, when the New Minster was moved to a site half a mile outside the North Gate of Winchester and founded anew as Hyde Abbey.

The king's last will and testament, drawn up sometime between 873 and 888, may still be read by us in its Old English original. In a preface Alfred writes of disagreements arising out of the inheritance of lands once owned by his brother, King Ethelred. He then declares that he laid this will and testament of his for judgment before the members of his West Saxon Council, begging "that none of them for love or fear of me should hesitate to declare the folkright, the customary law, in this matter, lest any man should say that I had been unfair toward my kinsmen, older or younger. Then," he continues, "they all duly judged and said that they could not think of a more just right than mine, nor find one written in the will. Now, they said, all that is described therein is again in thy hand. Do thou declare and give it to kinsman or to stranger, as shall be the more pleasing to thee."

The king, accordingly, divided out his lands and money among his family, his sons, his daughters, his nephews, his wife. Gifts of money, also, were left to each of his ealdormen; to his archbishop and his bishops; to the officials and personal attendants who gave him their service at court, to whom, as we learn here, he gave presents every Easter according to their ranking in his household. Legacy, too, was made of two hundred pounds "for me and for my father and for the friends for whom he prayed and I now pray," in the following division: fifty pounds to priests throughout his kingdom, fifty to poor "servants of God," doubtless in monasteries and houses of canons, fifty to the poor in special need, fifty to the church in which he should be laid to rest.

Further instructions bade that those who inherited the king's lands should leave these in legacy, if possible, to their male children; his grandfather Egbert had bequeathed his land to the "spear" side of his line, not to the "spindle" side. Finally, the king wrote, "I pray in the Name of God and His Saints that none of my kin or of my heirs vex any of those dependents for whom I have paid money. Let these choose whatever lord they will." The last sentence asked that "from my livestock, offering be made for my soul's need, as shall be possible and fitting and as you shall wish to give for me."

5

All down the centuries of English thought Alfred's name has lived, and yet with curious variations. Asser, who wrote his *Life*, declared him beloved of all men. We have seen the record of a belief that he might have been king of Wessex, had he so willed, even while his brother Ethelred was still living; we have seen his men full of joy when he once more met them for the great proving of battle after the solitude of Athelney. Yet, when he was dead, the same *Chronicle*, those annals fostered in his own kingdom, gave him no such burst of praise as they gave in the tenth century to his descendant, King Edgar.

Men of the Middle Ages and later held him, surely, in grateful memory. Late in the tenth century Aelfric, monk and priest of the Benedictine house of Cernel in Dorset, wrote of English people, "who neither knew nor had among their writings the teachings of the Gospel, except those who understood Latin, and except those books which King Alfred wisely turned from Latin into English, books still to be had." The Latin historians of England in the twelfth century—William of Malmesbury, Florence of Worcester, Simeon of Durham—waxed eloquent concerning Alfred's virtues in war and in peace. Simeon held him up as a model to the clergy of that time. Those same days, so the *Annals* of Winchester declare, revered his name as that of a sage full of wise sayings. It was even given to a collection of these sayings made about the end of the twelfth century by an unknown compiler and still in modern years extant under the title of "The Proverbs of Alfred." Others of these maxims were used as support by the Owl and the Nightingale in that famous contest of medieval poetry. In the sixteenth century Richard Hakluyt included the explorations of Ohthere and Wulfstan in his *Principall Navigations, Voiages and Discoveries of the English Nation;* in the seventeenth, Milton summed up Alfred's praise in his *History of Britain* and called him "the mirror of Princes."

English poetry, in general, has said surprisingly little of this man. The eighteenth century glorified him in minor epic. James Thomson collaborated in a masque for his honor and in *The Seasons* declared him "the best of Kings." To poets of the late years of that century and the early years of the nineteenth he symbolized, as was natural, the pride of England's liberty. Thus he stood for William Blake, in the "War Song for Englishmen," for Keats, for Shelley, and for Wordsworth, who also aptly described him as "this noble miser of his time." Longfellow in ballad form repeated "A Leaf from King Alfred's *Orosius.*"

It was, however, among the historians and essayists of the nineteenth century that his praise rose to panegyric. Now came the great rites of the thousandth anniversary of his birth; and, too, of his death, then held to have occurred in 901. That year of 1901 was marked with ritual of many and various celebrations, in church and in hall and on the green, by a vast assemblage of pilgrims at Winchester and at other centers of his fame. In the 1700's David Hume wrote of Alfred: "He seems, indeed, to be the model of that perfect character which, under the denomination of a sage or wise man, philosophers have been fond of delineating, rather as a fiction of their imagination than in hopes of ever seeing it really existing." Freeman later declared: "There is no other name in history to compare with his." In that same year of 1901, in an address at the Johns Hopkins University at

Baltimore, Frederic Harrison repeated the same: "Alfred, it is truly said, was the only perfect man of action in the annals of mankind. Without hyperbole, without boasting, we may say that the memory of Alfred is the most ancient, the most continuous, the most definite memory in all Christian history."

Yet Sharon Turner, even though his source was unreliable, in his *History of the Anglo-Saxons*, rebelled against this fervent stream: "It would be absurd for me," he wrote, "to offer any apology for having ventured to be the first in our history that has called the public attention to the faults of Alfred, whose life had been made one continued stream of panegyric." In 1896 George Cotterell, reviewing for *The Academy* a poem by the poet laureate, Alfred Austin, on this king, a poem called "England's Darling" in reminiscence of a medieval description, thus criticized Austin's choice of subject: "A hero pre-eminently fitted to be celebrated in song must possess qualities which neither history nor myth has associated with Alfred. He is too much of a paragon, too blameless, too unerring, too remote."

Such judgment rises from the fault, or, at least, the incompleteness, we may think, of Alfred's first biographer. For it is true that sometimes, after dwelling on the constant eulogy of Alfred in Asser's *Life*, one turns with a certain delight to Einhard's more complete picture of Charlemagne. The two kings, as has often been observed, were alike in many things: in their daily devotion to their faith, their care for their church, their renown as warriors, their zeal for order and rule, their passion for their own learning and for the learning of all their subjects, priests and lay, their love of their own native poetry, their "schools" for the sons of their nobles as well as for their own children, their enthusiasm for art and architecture, the curiosity which welcomed to their courts all who could tell them of things new and strange, the calling to their aid of scholars from without. Einhard is as keen for the praises of Charlemagne as Asser is for Alfred; yet we miss in Asser those frank, realistic descriptions of Charles, the king-emperor, riding along the roads of France with his sons by his side and his daughters "following in the rear"; trying to keep his daughters from the wooing of young men in his home; "almost hating" his doctors because they would not let him enjoy the roast meat which he loved, because they prescribed the boiled stuff which he hated; devoutly obeying his church but bitterly complaining of those many fast days, "so bad for his health"; loving to talk, even at times "a little garrulous"; rejoicing in sport with his friends in his great swimming pool at Aachen but stopping, as Alcuin tells us, in the midst of his sport to discuss a problem of theology. In contrast, Asser is one-sided in his picture of his king.

In 1441 King Henry the Sixth of England sent an envoy to Italy with a petition to the pope, Eugenius the Fourth, praying that King Alfred, "in whom the Lord has deigned to work miracles both in his life and in his death," might be canonized as saint. The petition was not granted. By that time Alfred and his deeds had grown dim in many minds; many problems, those of exile and schism among them, were pressing upon the pope; he knew nothing of "miracles" wrought through Alfred, in the ecclesiastic sense; and, moreover, the bond between

England and the Holy See was not at its closest in those years.

In the time of Alfred himself popes at Rome had repeatedly found cause to reproach the English for un-Christian ways. Pope John the Eighth not only wrote to King Burhred of Mercia of England's disregard of the church's marriage laws, but we have also a letter from him in reply to a lament from Ethelred, archbishop of Canterbury from 870 to 888, "exhorting and counselling you, my brother, as an apt servant of God, not only to place yourself in the path of your King [Alfred] as a wall of defense for the Lord's house, but to resist with vigor all who set themselves to perverse action therein." John said that he had also written to Alfred himself, but we do not have that letter, or the letter of Ethelred to the pope, nor do we know what fault of Alfred John had in mind. Probably, as we saw in the letters of Archbishop Fulk to Alfred and to Plegmund, the pope was referring to that heathen-"Christian" ritual of healing which, as in all countries, was so slow to die in England and which no king could summarily uproot. It may be noted here that this Ethelred was one of the witnesses of King Alfred's will; his lament does not, therefore, seem to have been permanent. Formosus, pope from 891 to 896, is also said to have written to the bishops of England, and in stern words, to the same effect: "When we heard that pagan rites had sprung up again in your land and that you had held silence, as dogs unable to bark, we had it in mind to smite you with the sword of separation from the body of the Church of God. But now, as our beloved Plegmund informs us, at last you have awakened." Yet, with all these rebukes, there is not the slightest evidence that King Alfred himself ever ceased to honor his church and her faith with all his heart and energy. We are even told that he longed to offer himself to prolonged bodily pain, if the Lord willed, for the discipline of his soul.

Nor does other criticism of this king bear marks of sober truth. The *Life* of St. Neot and the *Annals* of the priory known by his name declared that in the early years of Alfred's reign he was proud and haughty of spirit and refused to help the poor and distressed who sought him. For this, it was said, St. Neot reproved him, prophesying that great trouble would come upon him for his sin. The king, it was said, took no heed but rejected the holy man's words as foolish and false. In due time, however, grievous pain struck him again and again, and in his penitence the saint once more appeared, ready now to administer comfort and encouragement. The story bears all the signs of fiction, and, as we have remarked, its source is exceedingly unreliable.

Finally, we have a story from the Abbey of Abingdon in Berkshire. This house of God, we may think, rested upon Alfred's royal estate and suffered great harm in the raiding of Berkshire far and wide by the Danes in 871. It was only a little foundation, and its members were very few; but they complained bitterly that the king had robbed them: "piling evil upon evils," wrote their chronicler. "As Judas among the Twelve, he took away from us by force the land on which our house is built, known as the estate of Abingdon, with all the appurtenances belonging thereto." William of Malmesbury, in his account of the twelfth century, wrote that the king, "following

evil counsel, took the land for the use of himself and his."
No other evidence shows Alfred as a robber of monasteries. We have seen the reverse, indeed, in his endeavor
for Athelney and for Shaftesbury, in his gifts of money
to many other communities of Wessex. It may well be
that the land he took for his own use was that of his own
royal estate, in the neighborhood of the monastery but
not legally or permanently part of its holding, and that he
took it for cogent reasons of military defense against the
Danes.

Alfred still looks down upon his Wessex, down the old
street of Wantage and down the High Street of Winchester. His name still honors our tea rooms, our tower
of Stourhead, and our daffodils. The character which he
leaves with us is of one who met his duty with determination wherever he saw it, whether in pursuing Danish
enemies to their death or in driving his nobles to their
books and his magistrates to their duties; who knew himself to be king and lord, so declared by God, and punished with death those he found guilty of treason against
his crown; who fought sin and disorder, and ignorance,
which he accounted sin, throughout his lands; who sat
humbly with his books and with his counselors and
teachers to learn of them what he would hand on to
others of his charge; who in the midst of pain and cares
manifold followed day by day the vision of his soul; who
fed his people with a faithful and true heart and ruled
them prudently with all his power; to whom it was given
to deliver, well begun, the hope and object of his toil to
his followers for their achieving, whether in the gaining
of English liberty or in the creating of English prose or

in the carrying-on of the tradition of English law. Peter Hunter Blair in a few words has summed up Alfred's work: "In 878 this remarkable man had little left but an island fortress in the Somerset marshes, but ten years later, then a man rising forty, he ruled a wide kingdom and was learning Latin, so that he could make those translations of ancient books which can now be recognized as the foundations of English prose literature. It was a very sound instinct which bestowed on this man alone of all the kings of England the title of The Great."

BRIEF LIST OF *Books*

ANGLO-SAXON ENGLAND

CHADWICK, H. MUNRO. *Studies on Anglo-Saxon Institutions.* 1905.

CHAMBERS, R. W. *England before the Norman Conquest.* 1928.

FISHER, D. J. V. *Anglo-Saxon England* (in preparation).

HODGKIN, R. H. *A History of the Anglo-Saxons,* Vols. I–II. 1952.

HUNTER BLAIR, PETER. *An Introduction to Anglo-Saxon England.* 1956.

KNOWLES, M. D. (ed.). *The Heritage of Early Britain.* 1952.

Monumenta Historica Britannica, Vol. I, ed. H. PETRIE and T. SHARPE. 1848.

OMAN, SIR CHARLES. *England before the Norman Conquest.* 1949.

ROBERTSON, A. J. (ed. and trans.). *Anglo-Saxon Charters.* 1939.

SEARLE, W. G. *Anglo-Saxon Bishops, Kings, and Nobles.* 1899.

STENTON, SIR FRANK. *Anglo-Saxon England.* 1947.

———. *The Danes in England.* 1927.

———. *The Early History of the Abbey of Abingdon.* 1913.

———. *Latin Charters of the Anglo-Saxon Period.* 1955.

WHITELOCK, DOROTHY. *The Beginnings of English Society.* 1952.

———. (ed.). *English Historical Documents,* Vol. I, *ca.* 500–1042. 1955.

WRIGHT, C. E. *The Cultivation of Saga in Anglo-Saxon England.* 1939.

ANGLO-SAXON PROSE LITERATURE

ANDERSON, GEORGE K. *The Literature of the Anglo-Saxons.* 1949.

BRANDL, ALOIS, in HERMANN PAUL, *Gundriss der germanischen Philologie*, II (1901–9), 1062 ff.

CHAMBERS, R. W. "On the Continuity of English Prose from Alfred to More and His School," *Early English Text Society*, CLXXXVI (1932), lix f.

COOK, ALBERT S. *Biblical Quotations in Old English Prose Writers.* 1898.

MALONE, KEMP. "The Old English Period (to 1100)," in ALBERT C. BAUGH (ed.). *A Literary History of England*, pp. 1 ff. 1948.

POPE, JOHN. *English Literature before the Norman Conquest*, in the series "The Oxford History of English Literature" (in preparation).

SISAM, KENNETH. *Studies in the History of Old English Literature.* 1953.

THOMAS, P. G. "Alfred and the Old English Prose of His Reign," in *The Cambridge History of English Literature*, I, 97 ff. 1907.

ANGLO-SAXON LAW

ATTENBOROUGH, F. L. (ed. and trans.). *The Laws of the Earliest English Kings.* 1922.

LIEBERMANN, FELIX. *Die Gesetze der Angelsachsen*, Vols. I–III. 1903–16.

MAITLAND, FREDERIC W. *Domesday Book and Beyond.* 1897.

POLLOCK, SIR FREDERICK, and MAITLAND, FREDERIC W. *The History of English Law before the Time of Edward I*, Vol. I. 1898.

TURK, MILTON H. *The Legal Code of Ælfred the Great.* 1893.

ANGLO-SAXON ART AND ARCHITECTURE

BROOKE, GEORGE C. *English Coins from the Seventh Century to the Present Day.* 1950.

CLAPHAM, A. W. *English Romanesque Architecture before the Conquest.* 1930.

EARLE, JOHN. *The Alfred Jewel*. 1901.

KENDRICK, T. D. *Anglo-Saxon Art to A.D. 900*. 1938.

TALBOT RICE, D. *English Art, 871–1100*. 1952.

ANGLO-SAXON MEDICINE AND MAGIC

Bald's Leechbook. "Early English Manuscripts in Facsimile," ed. BERTRAM COLGRAVE; No. V, ed. C. E. WRIGHT. 1955.

COCKAYNE, OSWALD. *Leechdoms, Wortcunning, and Starcraft of Early England*, Vols. II and III. 1865–66.

GRATTAN, J. H. G., and SINGER, CHARLES. *Anglo-Saxon Magic and Medicine*. 1952.

GRENDON, FELIX. "The Anglo-Saxon Charms," *Journal of American Folklore*, XXII (1909), 105 ff.; reprinted 1930.

PAYNE, J. F. *English Medicine in the Anglo-Saxon Times*. 1904.

SINGER, CHARLES. *From Magic to Science*. 1928.

STORMS, G. *Anglo-Saxon Magic*. 1948.

KING ALFRED THE GREAT

ASSER. *Life of King Alfred, Together with the Annals of Saint Neots*, ed. W. H. STEVENSON. 1904. Trans. A. S. COOK. 1906. Trans. L. C. JANE. 1924.

BEAVEN, M. L. R. *English Historical Review*, XXXII (1917), 526 ff.; XXXIII (1918), 328 ff.

BOWKER, ALFRED (ed.). *Alfred the Great* (by various authors). 1899.

CONYBEARE, J. W. E. *Alfred in the Chroniclers*. 1914.

DOBLE, GILBERT H. *S. Neot*. "Cornish Saints" Series, No. 21. N.d.

GRIERSON, PHILIP. *English Historical Review*, LV (1940), 529 ff.

HARMER, FLORENCE E. *Select English Historical Documents of the Ninth and Tenth Centuries*. 1914.

HAYWARD, FRANK H. *Alfred the Great*. 1935.

LEES, BEATRICE A. *Alfred the Great: The Truth Teller*. 1915.

MAGOUN, FRANCIS P. *Modern Language Review*, XXXVII (1942), 409 ff.

MALONE, KEMP. "Oldest England": a lecture given at Oxford University in 1948 and printed in the *Emory University Quarterly*, Vol. V (1949).

MILES, LOUIS W. *King Alfred in Literature.* 1902.

PAULI, R. *König Ælfred und seine Stelle in der Geschichte Englands.* 1851. Trans. B. THORPE. 1853.

PLUMMER, CHARLES. *The Life and Times of Alfred the Great.* 1902.

SIMCOX, W. H. *English Historical Review,* I (1886), 218 ff.

STENTON, SIR FRANK. *English Historical Review,* XXIV (1909), 79 ff.; XXVII (1912), 512 f.

HISTORY OF WALES

CHADWICK, NORA K. (ed.). *Studies in Early British History.* 1954.

LLOYD, J. E. *A History of Wales,* Vols. I–II. 1939.

PHILLIMORE, EGERTON (ed.). *The Annales Cambriae, and Old-Welsh Genealogies from Harleian MS. 3859: Y Cymmrodor,* Vol. IX. 1888.

WADE-EVANS, A. W. (trans.). "The Annals of the Britons" (with his *Nennius's History of the Britons*). 1938.

WILLIAMS, A. H. *An Introduction to the History of Wales,* Vols. I–II. 1941–48.

CONTINENTAL HISTORY

GRIERSON, PHILIP. *Translations of the Royal Historical Society,* 4th Ser., XXIII (1941), 71 ff.

PREVITÉ-ORTON, C. W. *The Shorter Cambridge Medieval History.* Rev. ed. by PHILIP GRIERSON. 1952.

WALLACE-HADRILL, J. M. *The Barbarian West, 400–1000.* 1952.

THE VIKINGS

ELLIS, HILDA R. *The Road to Hel.* 1943.

KENDRICK, T. D. *History of the Vikings.* 1930.

MAWER, ALLEN. *The Vikings.* 1913.

OLRIK, AXEL. *Viking Civilization.* 1930.

SHETELIG, H., and FALK, H. *Scandinavian Archaeology*, trans.
E. V. GORDON. 1937.
TURVILLE-PETRE, G. *The Heroic Age of Scandinavia*. 1951.

The following scholars, among others, have written books,
dissertations, or articles on the Old English writings done by
or under King Alfred.

THE OLD ENGLISH "DIALOGUES" OF ST. GREGORY THE GREAT

Text: HANS HECHT: Grein-Wülker, Vol. V. 1900–1907.
Trans.: R. M. LUMIANSKY (unpublished Ph.D. thesis, University of North Carolina, 1942).
KELLER, WOLFGANG (*Quellen und Forschungen*, LXXXIV
[1900], 1 ff.); HOLTHAUSEN, F. (*Archiv f. d. Stud. d. neueren
Sprachen und Litt.*, CV [1900], 367 ff.); SCHERER, G., 1928;
HARTING, P. N. U. (*Neophilologus*, XXII [1937], 281 ff.);
TIMMER, B. J., 1934.

THE WRITINGS OF KING ALFRED

WÜLFING, J. ERNST, 1894–1901; KOEPPEL, E. (*Beiblatt zur
Anglia*, XIX [1908], 330 ff.); RAUERT, M., 1910; BROWNE,
G. F., 1920; BORINSKI, LUDWIG, 1934.

THE OLD ENGLISH VERSION OF ST. GREGORY THE GREAT
"CURA PASTORALIS"

Text and Trans.: HENRY SWEET, *Early English Text Society*,
Vols. XLV and L. 1871–72. ELLIOTT VAN KIRK DOBBIE, *The
Anglo-Saxon Minor Poems*. 1942.
DEWITZ, ALBERT, 1889; WACK, G., 1889; KERN, J. H. (PAUL UND
BRAUNE, *Beiträge*, XVI [1892], 554 ff.; *Anglia*, XXXIII
[1910], 270 ff.); HOLTHAUSEN, F. (*Archiv*, CVI [1901],
346 f.); JOST, KARL (*Anglia*, XXXVII [1913], 63 ff.); KLAEBER, FR. (*Anglia*, XLVII [1923], 53 ff.).

THE OLD ENGLISH BEDE

Text: JACOB SCHIPPER: Grein-Wülker, Vol. IV. 1899.
Text and Trans.: THOMAS MILLER, *Early English Text Society*, Vols. XCV, XCVI, CX, and CXI. 1890–98.

ZUPITZA, JULIUS (*Zeitschrift f. deutsches Alterthum*, XXX [1886], 185 f.); SCHMIDT, AUGUST, 1889; PEARCE, J. W. (*Proceedings of the Modern Language Association*, VIII [1893], vi ff.); MATHER, FRANK JEWETT (*Modern Language Notes*, IX [1894], 154–55); MILLER, THOMAS (*Quellen und Forschungen*, LXXVIII [1896], 1 ff.); SCHIPPER, J. (*Sitz. ber. phil. hist. Cl.* [Wien, 1898]); KLAEBER, FR. (*Publications of the Modern Language Association*, XV [1900], lxxii f.; *Anglia*, XXV [1902], 257 ff.; XXVII [1904], 243 ff., 399 ff.); DEUTSCHBEIN, M., 1900, and PAUL UND BRAUNE (*Beiträge*, XXVI [1901], 169 ff.); HART, J. M. (*Furnivall Miscellany* [1901], pp. 150 ff.); FIJN VAN DRAAT, P. (*Anglia*, XXXIX [1916], 319 ff.); POTTER, SIMEON (*Mémoires, Soc. Royale* [Prague, 1931], pp. 1 ff.).

THE OLD ENGLISH OROSIUS

Text: HENRY SWEET, *Early English Text Society*, Vol. LXXIX, No. 1. 1883.

Trans.: B. THORPE in R. PAULI (trans.) *Life of Alfred the Great*, pp. 239 ff. 1853.

SCHILLING, H., 1886; GEIDEL, H., 1904; KOEPPEL, E. (*Beiblatt zur Anglia*, XIX [1908], 332–33); LOGEMAN, H. (*Englische Studien*, XL [1909], 464 f.); NANSEN, F., 1911; LABORDE, E. D. (*Geographical Journal*, LXII [1923], 133 ff.); HÜBENER, G. (*Englische Studien*, LX [1925], 37 ff.; *Speculum*, VI [1931], 296 ff., 428 ff.); CRAIGIE, SIR WILLIAM (*Journal of English and Germanic Philology*, XXIV [1925], 396 f.); MALONE, KEMP (*Modern Language Review*, XX [1925], 1 ff.; XXIII [1928], 336 ff.; XXV [1930], 78 ff.; *Speculum*, V [1930], 139 ff.; VIII [1933], 67 ff.; *Studies in Philology*, University of North Carolina, XXVIII [1931], 574 ff.); KIRKMAN, ANN (*Modern Language Review*, XXV [1930], 1 ff.); CROSS, S. H. (*Speculum*, VI [1931], 296 ff.); ROSS, ALAN, University of Leeds, 1940; EKBLOM, R. (*Studia neophilologica*, XIV [1942], 115 ff.); MAGOUN, FRANCIS P. (*Scandinavian Studies*, XVIII [1944], 163 f.); WHITING, B. J. (*Philological Quarterly*, XXIV [1945], 218 ff.).

Text: W. J. SEDGEFIELD. 1899.

Trans.: W. J. SEDGEFIELD. 1900.

LEICHT, ALFRED, 1882, and *Anglia*, VI (1883), 126 ff.; VII (1884), 176 ff.; HARTMANN, M. (*Anglia*, V [1882], 411 ff.); ZIMMER-MANN, O., 1882; NAPIER, A. S. (*Zeitschrift f. deutsches Alt.*, XXXI [1887], 52 ff.); PAUL UND BRAUNE (*Beiträge*, XXIV [1899], 245 f.); COSSACK, A. H., 1889; SCHEPSS, G. (*Archiv*, XCIV [1895], 149 ff.); FÖRSTER, MAX (*Archiv*, CVI [1901], 342 f.); KRÄMER, E. (*Bonner Beiträge zur Anglistik*, VIII [1902], 1 ff.); KRAWUTSCHKE, A., 1902; KLAEBER, FR. (*Modern Language Notes*, XVIII [1903], 241 ff.; *Anglia*, XLVII [1923], 53 ff.); FEHLAUER, F., 1908; KOEPPEL, E. (*Beiblatt zur Anglia*, XIX [1908], 330 ff.); STEWART, H. F. (*Journal of Theological Studies*, XVII [1916], 22 ff.); KERN, J. H. (*Neophilologus*, VIII [1923], 295 ff.); KRAPP, GEORGE P., 1932; SCHMIDT, K. H., 1934; PATCH, HOWARD R., 1935.

THE OLD ENGLISH VERSION OF ST. AUGUSTINE: "SOLILOQUIES"

Text: W. ENDTER: Grein-Wülker, Vol. XI. 1922. H. L. HARGROVE, *Yale Studies in English*, Vol. XIII (1902). W. H. HULME, *Englische Studien*, XVIII (1893), 331 ff.; XIX (1894), 470.

Trans.: H. L. HARGROVE, *Yale Studies in English*, Vol. XXII (1904).

HUBBARD, F. G. (*Modern Language Notes*, IX [1894], 321 ff.); HULME, W. H., 1894; WÜLFING, J. E. (*Englische Studien*, XX [1895], 335 ff.); JOST, KARL (*Beiblatt zur Anglia*, XXXI [1920], 259 ff., 280 ff.; XXXII [1921], 8 ff.); POTTER SIMEON, *Philologica*, 1949, pp. 25 ff.

THE OLD ENGLISH PROSE PSALMS

Text: J. W. BRIGHT and R. L. RAMSAY. 1907. R. L. RAMSAY (*American Journal of Philology*, XLI [1920], 147 ff.).

WICHMANN, J. (*Anglia*, XI [1889], 39 ff.); BRUCE, J. D., 1894, and *Modern Language Notes*, VIII (1893), 72 ff.; GRATTAN,

J. H. G. (*Modern Language Review,* IV [1909], 185 ff.);
Bromwich, J. I'a (*H. M. Chadwick Memorial Studies,* ed.
Sir Cyril Fox and Bruce Dickins, pp. 289 ff. 1950).

THE "ANGLO-SAXON CHRONICLE"

Texts: B. Thorpe, Rolls Series, Text and Translation, 1861.
J. Earle and C. Plummer, 1892–99. A. H. Smith, 1951.
Trans.: G. N. Garmonsway, 1955.
Stenton, Sir Frank: *Essays Presented to Thomas Frederick Tout,* pp. 15 ff. 1925.

WORKS NOT BY KING ALFRED OR ASCRIBED TO HIM ON UNCERTAIN EVIDENCE

In the twelfth century Ailred of Rievaulx (*PL,* Vol. CXCV, col. 722) and the *Book of Ely* (Vol. I, ed. D. J. Stewart, 1848, p. 81) attributed to King Alfred a translation of the Bible. On this see Philip Grierson, *English Historical Review,* LV (1940), 552, n. 2; R. M. Wilson, *The Lost Literature of Medieval England,* p. 73. 1952.

The *Old English Martyrology* was a translation, made in England during the later ninth century, from a Latin text now lost. This translation may have been made in Mercia. A very reasonable theory, however, suggests that it was made under King Alfred, late in his reign, by one of his scholars from Mercia (see Celia Sisam, *Review of English Studies,* N.S., IV [1953], 209 ff.).

For the so-called *Proverbs of Alfred* see W. W. Skeat, 1907; Helen P. South, 1931; Kemp Malone, in Baugh, p. 96; R. M. Wilson, p. 73, also in *Early Middle English Literature,* 1939, pp. 189 f.; Ailred of Rievaulx, *PL,* Vol. CXCV, col. 722; *Annales monastici,* II, ed. Luard, 10; O. S. Andersson Arngart, 1942–55.

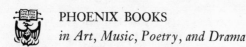

PHOENIX BOOKS
in Art, Music, Poetry, and Drama

PHOENIX POETS